**DETAIL** Practice

# Lighting Design

Principles
Implementation
Case Studies

ULRIKE BRANDI LICHT

Edition Detail

Authors:
Christina Augustesen, Architect
Ulrike Brandi Licht GmbH, Hamburg

Ulrike Brandi, Director
Ulrike Brandi Licht GmbH, Hamburg

Udo Dietrich, PhD
Büro für Bauphysik, Gebäudesimulation und
Integrales Planen, Hamburg

Annette Friederici, MA Cultural Studies
Ulrike Brandi Licht GmbH, Hamburg

Christoph Geissmar-Brandi, PhD
Ulrike Brandi Licht GmbH, Hamburg

Peter Thule Kristensen, Architect, PhD
Assistant at the School of History
and Theory of Architecture,
School of Architecture – Royal Danish
Academy of Fine Arts, Copenhagen

Merete Madsen, Architect, PhD
Assistant at the School of Daylight Research,
School of Architecture – Royal Danish
Academy of Fine Arts, Copenhagen,

Anja Storch, Lawyer/Mediator, Hamburg

Burkhard Wand, Dipl.-Ing.
Ulrike Brandi Licht GmbH, Hamburg

Editor:
Andrea Wiegelmann, Dipl.-Ing.

Editorial Staff:
Nicola Kollmann, Dipl.-Ing.
Christina Schulz, Architect

Drawings:
Andrea Saiko, Dipl.-Ing.

Translation:
Caroline Ahrens, Esther Mallach p. 84 – 89

© 2006 Institut für internationale
Architektur-Dokumentation GmbH & Co. KG,
Munich

An Edition DETAIL book

ISBN-10: 3-7643-7493-4
ISBN-13: 978-3-7643-7493-8

Printed on acid-free paper made from cellulose
bleached without the use of chlorine.

Typesetting and production:
Peter Gensmantel, Andrea Linke,
Roswitha Siegler, Simone Soesters

Printed by:
Wesel-Kommunikation, Baden-Baden

This book is also available in a German
language edition (ISBN 3-920034-12-0).

A CIP catalogue record for this book is
available from the Library of Congress,
Washington D.C., USA

Bibliographic information published by
Die Deutsche Bibliothek
Die Deutsche Bibliothek lists this publication in
the Deutsche Nationalbibliographie; detailed
bibliographic data is available on the internet at
http://dnb.ddb.de

Institut für internationale
Architektur-Dokumentation GmbH & Co. KG
Sonnenstrasse 17,
80331 Munich, Germany
Tel.: +49 89 38 16 20-0
Fax: +49 89 39 86 70
Internet: www.detail.de

Distribution Partner:
Birkhäuser – Publishers for Architecture
P.O. Box 133, CH-4010 Basel, Switzerland
Tel.: +41 61 205 07 07
Fax: +41 61 205 07 92
email: sales@birkhauser.ch
http://www.birkhauser.ch

**DETAIL** Practice
Lighting Design

## Can one design light?

The free internet encyclopaedia Wikipedia, currently one of the most topical and intriguing collections of knowledge, states in its German version:
"Planning is the intellectual process of creating a design with elements of varying relative and intrinsic significance: the applications and the comprehension of planning are thus also variable. As a central tenet, the essence of planning can be described as the bringing into being of concepts that are both target-oriented and value-assessed.
If planning is to be of practical use, two further criteria must be fulfilled: it must be based on existing or feasible resources to allow for its realisation, and it must be allotted a timescale within which it is to be either realised or abandoned.
The purpose of planning is to create clarity. Planning, the creation of target-oriented, value-assessed concepts with regard to time and resources, is carried out for the purpose of optimising the progression of a future series of events. (Linked) examples are: landscape architecture, urban planning, regional planning, development control planning and construction planning."

How does this apply to the planning of light?
ibidem:
"Light is that part of electromagnetic radiation that is visible to the human eye, the electromagnetic waves within the frequency range 380–780 nanometre (750 nm: red, 400 nm: violet/blue). The visible spectrum is part of the electromagnetic spectrum. The differing sensitivities of pigment molecules (blue, green-yellow, orange-red) in the rod cells of the human eye to different wavelengths forms the basis of photometry. While cone cells are responsible for colour vision, rod cells in the retina register the luminous intensity by means of splitting rhodopsin within the retinal molecules on reception of light photons..."

Is this the sole frame of reference for the planning of light?

The first comprehensive German encyclopaedia, Zedlers Lexikon, "the large complete universal encyclopaedia of all sciences and arts, that have hitherto been invented and improved by the human mind and wit (...) Leipzig 1732" takes a different standpoint. There is no entry for planning, but the following for light:

"Licht, ist vornehmlich zweyerley Art
Licht, Lat. Lux
Licht, Kertze
Licht, wird in heiliger Schrifft genennet
Licht heisset bey dem Baue die öffnung
Licht, das helle Theil eines Gemählde
Licht, ein brennendes und scheinendes war
Licht, der Dämmerung ähnliches
Licht, ewiges
Licht, Stärckedesselbigen
Licht, da niemand zukommen kann, darinen
Licht, das da scheinet in einem dunckeln
Licht hieß Gott aus dem Finsterniß hervorleuchten
Licht ist dein Kleid
Licht ist Gott
Licht ist noch eine kleine Zeit bey euch
Licht ist süß
Licht kommet, dein
Licht lasset leuchten vor denen Leuten, ec.
Licht des Lebens
Licht meiner Augen ist nicht bey mir
Licht muß dem Gerechten immer wieder
Licht scheidete Gott von der Finsterniß, ec.
Licht scheinet in der Finsterniß
Licht versäumen
Licht wird's seyn um den Abend
Licht und Heil ist mir der Herr, vor wem ec.
Licht und Recht
Licht der Welt seyd ihr
Licht vom Himmel erleuchtete
Licht werden
Licht wird hervor brechen wie die Morgen-Röthe"

Light has many meanings
Light, Latin lux
Light from candles
Light is referred to in the Holy Bible
Etc. etc.

This collection of knowledge finds manifold poetic expressions to describe the phenomenon of light. In total the author lists 32 incidences of light in the encyclopaedia. One can sense how far light dominated life in those days and how it was synonymous with human life and nature. Hence, his final sentence is: "Light will erupt like dawn".
This conception is still easier to understand. The authors of this book are in fact describing the conceptual uses of daylight and artificial light in today's building processes, beginning in the 20th century. For this reason, we have begun our overview with the last chapter of this volume. Merete Madsen and Peter Thule Kristensen draw on examples to chronologically trace the use of daylight as a building material in the 20th and early 21st century.
Anja Storch, a lawyer specialising in planning law, writes about the dominating role of costs and contracts in the planning process.
The latest event in the musefication of the automobile is to be found at the new Mercedes Benz Museums in Stuttgart, designed by UN-Studio, combining artificial exhibition lighting with natural illumination.
A brief guide to the procedures of designing artificial light is included. Case studies describe the necessary steps, from the first considerations of light in a building to the completed project design. The previous chapter examines new trends in lighting design in the context of the interdisciplinary automation of buildings.
In her analysis of a church, Christina Augustesen shows how light and shadow can be the central defining elements of spaces.
The combined use of natural and artificial light as a means of reducing energy consumption while increasing comfort levels was a requirement of the design brief for a new public utilities building in Schönebeck. The case study introduces the relevant systems and components.
Udo Dietrich explains in his long and coherent piece how daylight can be integrated into the design of new developments – a practical summary, not seen before in this form.
And finally, natural light has a great bearing on our well-being, as Annette Friederici and Burkhard Wand describe in their article.
We hope the book will help to create more awareness for the use of light in architecture.

Hamburg, May 2005
Ulrike Brandi
Christoph Geissmar-Brandi

Right: Galerie de L'Evolution,
Museum of Natural History, Paris, renovation 1994
Not implemented was the design for a daylight ceiling that projected the path of the sun in different seasons to create changing light ambience in the interior. The final proposal utilises artificial light to protect the exhibits (see pp. 82/83).

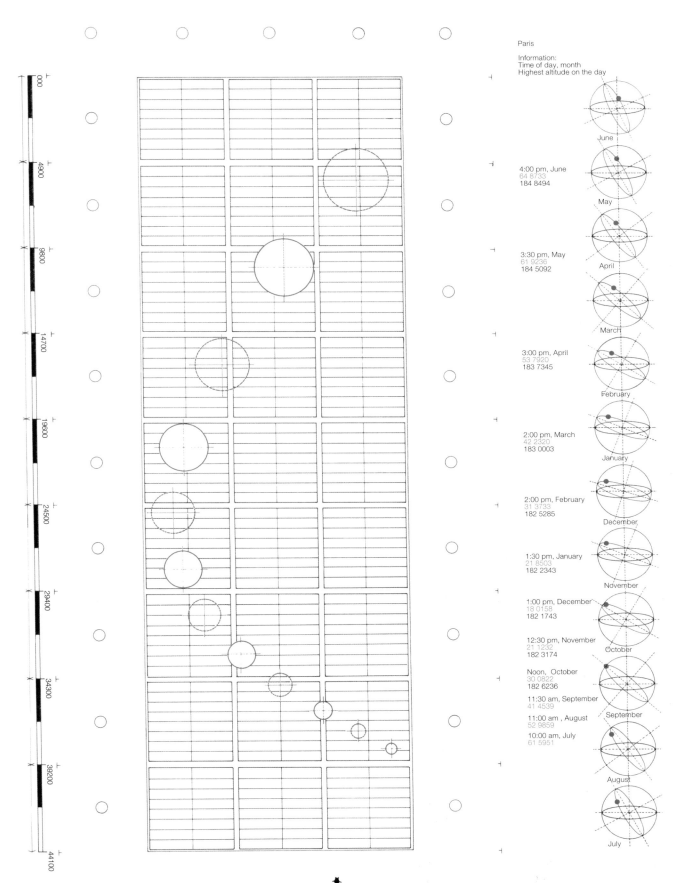

Paris

Information:
Time of day, month
Highest altitude on the day

June

4:00 pm, June
64 8733
184 8494

May

3:30 pm, May
61 9236
184 5092

April

3:00 pm, April
53 7920
183 7345

March

2:00 pm, March
42 2320
183 0003

February

2:00 pm, February
31 3733
182 5285

January

1:30 pm, January
21 8503
182 2343

December

1:00 pm, December
18 0158
182 1743

12:30 pm, November
21 1232
182 3174

November

Noon, October
30 0822
182 6236

11:30 am, September
41 4539

October

11:00 am , August
52 9859

10:00 am, July
61 5951

September

August

July

000
4900
9800
14700
19600
24500
29400
34300
39200
44100

# Daylight and Well-Being

Annette Friederici
Burkhard Wand

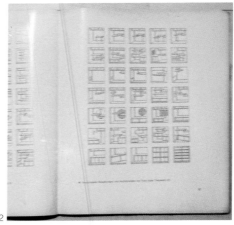

### No life without light

From birth, man strives towards light. It is the basis of all existence on our planet. Without light we cannot breathe, nor see or perceive colour (Figure 1). As the source of energy for photosynthesis, light is the primary source of life for man. Via the sensory system it controls the processing activities of important information. Furthermore, life science research has identified the photo-biological characteristics of light and emphasised its role in human well-being. The visual system, in complex processes, enables not only our spatial orientation but also controls motoric and hormonal activities which help the development of our three-dimensional perception.

Knowledge about the effects of daylight – as a controlling element of various psycho-physiological processes in organisms – has changed and expanded established concepts of daylight planning in buildings. This necessitates an integrated approach incorporating aspects of architecture, lighting technology and life science.

### Psychological effects of daylight

Human dependency on light and the positive effects of natural light on our health becomes apparent only when we are deprived of light or exposed to excess quantities of light. Through the human eye and skin photobiological processes are triggered which have an effect on our physical and psychological constitution. Poor light conditions lead to fatigue of the eyes and brain (Figure 2).

The type of light also influences the psychological constitution of man. A well known example of this is the influence of daylight with respect to its seasonal progression. Short, dull days in winter often have a negative effect on our mood. Studies by the Research Foundation of Lighting and Health in the Netherlands have

shown that roughly 70 % of the population feel minor depressive mood swings. They also confirmed that additional light at the workplace relieves these symptoms which, in turn, has a positive effect on well-being, and hence on performance. Scientists call the chronic form of winter depression Seasonal Affective Disorder (SAD); approximately 3 % of the population are affected. It can be successfully treated with a light therapy during the dark winter months.

Light is the most important time regulator of the human biorhythm. The alternation of day and night brought about by the rotation of the earth in a 24-hour cycle (circadian rhythm) activates the production of hormones in the human body (Figure 3). Recent scientific studies have found that the circadian rhythm influences our sense of time much more than social factors such as working or eating rhythms. The pineal gland's secretion of the hormone melatonin (sleeping hormone) is determined by the illumination level, the length of exposure and the spectral composition of the light reflected onto the retina. In work environments the optimisation of production processes has led to extending working hours into the night (more efficient use of production facilities) and to building workplaces largely without windows (maximum area utilisation and production optimisation). Artificial lighting systems were developed and replaced daylight with static light. This, however, cannot compensate for a lack of ultraviolet rays or the liveliness of sunlight (Figure 5 a, b). One of the diseases typical of recent times is rickets, caused by a lack of sunlight. Insufficient levels of ultraviolet sunlight (280 nm – 320 nm) reduces the human skin's production of vitamin D, which regulates the absorption of calcium from food and its uptake by the bones. The result is the softening of the bones which can lead to

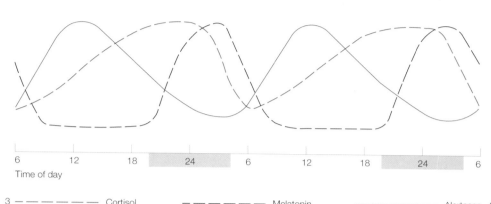

6    12    18    24    6    12    18    24    6

Time of day

3 — — — — — Cortisol     — — — — — Melatonin     ———— Alertness 4

cessation of growth, or even bone deterioration.

The lack of daylight is second only to air-conditioning as the leading cause of SBS, Sick Building Syndrome. The World Health Organisation coined the term in 1983 to describe the negative effects of the built environment that are not related to a specific physical illness. A study by A. and G. Çakir proved that the typical symptoms of SBS – headaches, fatigue, numbness and irritation of the eyes – increase in proportion to the use of artificial lighting. The ailments increase the further the workplace is located towards the centre of the room, while higher levels of daylight have shown to improve performance. In addition the phenomenon of psychological glare suggests that artificial lighting, even if it is installed to standard specifications, cannot replace the quality of daylight.

Psychological glare is the manifestation of a subjectively felt disturbance caused by a great disparity of light intensity in the field of vision. Glare caused by brightly lit surfaces, or luminaires themselves, can impair our visual performance and contribute to deterioration in our well-being, while generally, we perceive glare caused by sunlight as pleasant. The reason for this is not yet known, but it can be presumed that glare from daylight is less disturbing because it also conveys information (time of day, season, weather conditions, etc.).

### Qualities of natural light

What distinguishes daylight from artificial lighting? What are its specific qualities? The trend continues in which the human being is exposed to only a fraction of the daylight a life in closer contact with nature would provide. In many situations we instinctively turn towards daylight: when we look out of the window in the office, or draw the first breath upon leaving artificially lit, windowless rooms. The standard illuminance of 500 lx at the workplace is sometimes perceived as too bright, whereas out-of-doors 5000 lx seem pleasantly dark. This example illustrates where the deficits of entirely artificially lit spaces lie.

The dynamics of daylight have a stimulating effect on us. Light is modulated in many ways, deformed and structured, before being reflected onto the retina, as light carrying secondary information. We never see the total amount of light hitting an object (illuminance), but only the light reflected at a specific point (luminance), the amount and composition being determined by the properties of the lit surface (see also pp. 17, 18). We receive information about the shape, colour and spatiality of our surroundings from brightness and colour contrasts (Figure 7). Resultant are the following dynamic components of daylight which are dependant upon the spectral transparency of the atmosphere of the location (changing climatic conditions, particle content of the air) and the respective seasonal and daily path of the sun.

1   Sunflowers, turned towards the sun. Without light we cannot breathe, cannot see or perceive colours.
2   Poor lighting conditions lead to fatigue of the eyes and mind. We can no longer concentrate, letters swim in front of our eyes, and words turn into hieroglyphs.
3   2 × 24-hour diagram of different circadian rhythms in the human body
4   Light pollution at night in the port of Hamburg. In large industrialised nations night is turned into day by artificial light. This disturbs the ecological and biological equilibrium.
5   a Spectral composition of sunlight
    b Spectrum of a fluorescent lamp without UV-B radiation

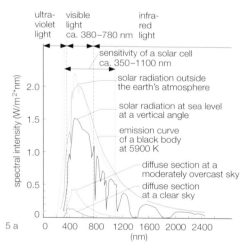

ultra-violet light    visible light ca. 380–780 nm    infra-red light

sensitivity of a solar cell ca. 350–1100 nm

solar radiation outside the earth's atmosphere

solar radiation at sea level at a vertical angle

emission curve of a black body at 5900 K

diffuse section at a moderately overcast sky

diffuse section at a clear sky

spectral intensity (W/m²*nm)

5 a    0   400   800   1200   1600   2000   2400   (nm)

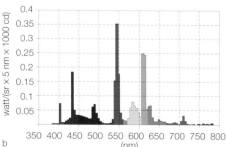

watt/(sr × 5 nm × 1000 cd)

350 400 450 500 550 600 650 700 750 800 (nm)

b

6 a     b

*Brightness*

As a consequence of these previously mentioned influences, the outdoor illuminance can vary between levels exceeding 100000 lx on a sunny summer's day, to below 5000 lx on a cloudy day in winter. We refer to a variation in the brightness of daylight although what we really see is the luminance of the surface onto which the light falls. These absolute, quantifiable values (luminance in candela per m²) are only of minor importance to our perception of brightness.

How bright or how dark we perceive an area to be does not depend on the inten-

sity of the physical stimulus (luminance). It is always the relative brightness of different areas to one another that triggers a sensation of brightness. The following example illustrates this:

If one looks at a dark building facade in direct sunlight and a white sheet of paper on a desk lit to standard specification, the physical sensation caused by the dark building facade will be much more intense than that by the paper (Figure 6 a, b). But the facade looks black and the paper white, because in the first case we have a relatively weak stimulus

blue sky:
4000 cd/m²

overcast sky:
6000 cd/m²

sun:
1600000000 cd/m²

illuminance of the overcast sky:
5000–20000 lx

illuminance of sunshine:
20000–100000 lx

7

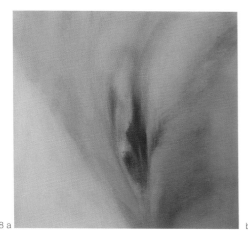
8 a

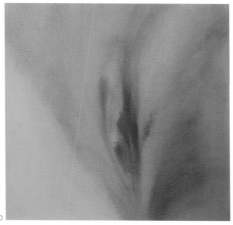
b

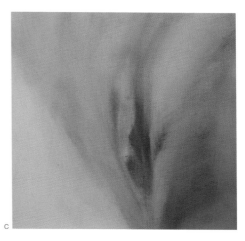
c

in very bright daylight and in the second, the strongest possible stimulus in artificial light.

*Colour and the spectral composition of daylight*
The sun is the source of natural light. Sunlight entering the earth's atmosphere is scattered mainly in the range of the short-wave blue end of the spectrum. This is why the sky looks blue. Depending on the weather conditions it may look white-grey with an overcast sky (~5000 K) or clear blue with a cloudless sky (~100000 K). Sunrise and sunset appear red to us because the light must travel a longer distance through the denser strata of the atmosphere closer to the surface of the earth. The blue part of sunlight is scattered while mainly the long-wave light (red) passes through.
Despite different colour temperatures (measured in K = Kelvin), we perceive daylight as being more or less white. It seems that our visual system can assess the spectral properties of the incoming rays and compensate for its effect on the appearance of objects. This phenomenon of perception is called colour constancy (Figure 8 a–c).

*Light direction*
Daylight can be subdivided into directed light (near parallel light with an apex angle of only 0.5°) and diffuse light from the sky (scattered light) occurring on days with a clear or overcast sky. Shadows, determined by the effects of contrast, are also a product of the light direction (next to other influences, such as type of light, environment and observer). Shadow is an important factor in the perception of space and objects. Depending on the proportion of directional sunlight and diffuse daylight, one can, apart from dark-light contrasts, observe coloured shadow on lit objects, with the colour tone corresponding to the complementary colour of the light (Figure 9).

6   a, b   If one looks at a dark building facade in direct sunlight and a white sheet of paper on a desk lit to standard specification, the physical sensation caused by the dark building facade is much more intense than that by the paper, but the facade looks darker and the paper bright white.
7   Examples of the luminance of the sky (cd/m²) and related illuminance (lx) on the ground. However, we do not perceive illuminance as brightness, but as luminance. This is the part of light from the sky and sunlight that is reflected by the objects onto which it falls and then to the eye. At an equal illuminance on the ground we perceive daylight, as different levels of brightness (luminance) depending on the reflective properties of the surface lit. The grass looks darker than the water – under an overcast sky there is less contrast than in sunshine.
8   a   Object in daylight (blue tinge)
     b   Object in artificial light (yellow tinge)
     c   Object as perceived by the human eye.
9   Claude Monet, Grainstack, 1891. The painting shows the coloured shadows described in the text.

9

11

**Daylight utilisation in buildings**

Light enables us to experience interior spaces – for this reason lighting design is one of the essential components of architecture. The lighting concept determines the appearance of a space which will change through the manipulation of light. Within seconds, we obtain visual information about the space we are in, without the trouble of having to feel our way around. The response we have to a space, any sympathy or antipathy it may trigger in us, is not just a result of the sensation caused by light hitting the retina, but is related to other sensations that respond associatively during visual perception, and significantly contribute to the form of the visual information. Space and user have a reciprocal effect on one another. The conscious perception of a space is an abstraction, a creative process that is influenced by our emotional condition, experience and knowledge just as much as by noise, scent and colour. Until the worldwide introduction of electric light just over 100 years ago, all built spaces were reliant on daylight. The invention of the fluorescent lamp in the mid-20th century brought better efficacy in comparison to the light bulb, and hence improved economic efficiency. This led to a change in lighting concepts. Particularly during the 1980s many virtually daylight-free open plan offices were built with centrally controlled (artificial) lighting and ventilation systems. Today, the trend is towards the utilisation of daylight, because it has been recognised that instead of improving productivity, continuous, constant lighting has a negative impact on the health of employees, reducing performance and motivation. In private homes and in public workplaces alike, the reliance on a combination of daylight and artificial lighting is used to augment visual performance, visual comfort and economic efficiency. Lighting has to satisfy the visual and the non-image-forming needs. To facilitate good orientation at home and in the workplace, tiring, laboratory-like and uniform illumination, or dynamic light effects causing irritation, should be avoided. Identification with our environment is one of the essential criteria for our physical, mental and spiritual well-being. Functional, aesthetic and emotional aspects are interdependent. Concepts that form synergies in the use of daylight and artificial light are much sought after.
It should be noted that the use of daylight in architecture is a subtractive process since only a fraction of available light reaches the interior of a building, while illumination with artificial light is an additive process "in which lumen by lumen the interior of the space must be created" (Volkher Schultz).

The following section includes several examples of successful modern lighting concepts that make good use of the qualities of daylight while effectively supplementing these with artificial light.

*Example: Workplace*
Light in the workplace, whether in the administration or production sector, should provide a healthy, safe and comfortable working environment. In consideration of these three factors, the following daylight and artificial lighting criteria for good and efficient visual performance can be listed:

- illumination
- uniformity (at the place of work)
- luminance conditions in the field of vision
- avoidance of glare
- light distribution (in interior spaces)
- colour properties of light

Frequent accidents, errors and general performance are directly related to the quality of lighting. For a working person to maintain a constant level of productivity, he requires short periods of relaxation in which other sensory stimuli relieve monotony; he thus avoids both physical and mental symptoms of fatigue. Generally, in office spaces with daylighting, sufficient light is available from the windows. Night work or shift work, on the other hand, entails working against the natural biorhythm. American scientists have found that at an illumination level above 2 000 lx the secretion of melatonin (sleeping hormone) may be suppressed or postponed, while an illumination level of 500 lx, commonly found in offices, does not affect physical well-being. A bright working environment increases physical activity, and hence is one of the factors contributing to improved performance. An excess amount of light, on the other hand, can have the opposite effect, exacerbating fatigue. Depending on the work setting, individual lighting requirements and superordinate interests should be taken into consideration to reach the best results.

10

11

12

*Example: Hospital*

It seems strange that, although the Roman architectural theoretician Vitruvius, in the 1st century BC, searched for solutions to apply the knowledge of the healing properties of light to architecture, the therapeutical effect of light in hospital building was completely, or partly ignored for many decades in the 20th century. Hospitals are dominated by highly technical medical apparatuses that are able to dissect the patient into single functional entities, without seeing the human being as a whole – neglecting the interplay of psyche and soma. Recently architects and designers have focussed on a holistic approach in their interior design and

architecture. Many hospital operators have recognised – in part due to economic pressure – that the so-called "well-being factors" have a positive influence on the healing process. Carefully planned use of light as a therapeutic tool is one of these factors.

Better services and comfort create a stimulating environment, reducing the need for drugs and shortening the time spent in hospital. A well-balanced design of daylight and artificial lighting is not only beneficial to patients but also to the hospital staff. The harmonious light ambience enhances the well-being of everyone, reduces stress and fear, and creates an atmosphere of comfort.

State Insurance Institution of the City of Hamburg
Architects: Schweger and Partners, Hamburg
Lighting design: ULRIKE BRANDI LICHT
The new administrative building for the insurance institution is a clear architectural composition. Low-key design and high functionality determine the appearance of interior spaces in which the light is quite naturally subordinate.

10   In the foyer clear "islands of light" emphasise certain areas. The eye-catcher is the wall (a wash of light) opposite the entrance and the view of the courtyard (sidelight on plants). The main type of luminaire is a round downlight recessed into the ceiling. A complex technical light control system is hidden beyond: depending on the requirements, reflectors produce focussed beams, wide beams or asymmetrical light cones creating a wide repertoire of light scenes.

11, 13   Photograph and floor plan show a standard office space on the west side. The glazing extends nearly to the full height of the room, offering generous views to the outside and providing optimum daylight delivery. A second glass skin, ventilated from behind, forms a buffer zone in front of the inner glazing in which a perforated Venetian blind is installed as protection from heat gain and glare. It directs daylight onto the ceiling and into the depth of the room (also see pp. 46–47). Artificial light is subordinate to the daylight concept: for the workplaces luminaire standards with a high degree of indirect light are placed close to the windows, exploiting the reflective properties of the ceiling.

12   Downlights in the cafeteria provide uniform light across the area, which is not specific to the tables. Small pendant luminaires create "light stimuli" and light accents.

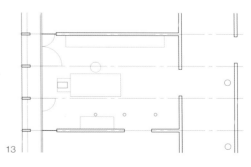

13

Industrial complex B. Braun, Melsungen
Architects: James Stirling, Michael Wilford
in association with Walter Nägeli
Lighting design: ULRIKE BRANDI LICHT
Lighting concept: Tension is invigorating – areas are differentiated by setting off daylight against artificial light.

14 Dispatch hall (1st construction phase, 1992)
15 Office space in the extension building, 2001
The "Office Concept 2010" envisions flexible, paper-free workplaces that are different in character and selected by the users on a daily basis. The light contributes to the specific atmosphere of each workplace. Open extroverted zones with a view are contrasted by closed introverted spaces in which visual stimuli are reduced.
16 Foyer of the administration building (first construction phase, 1992)

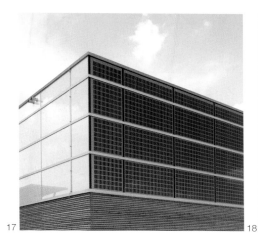 

17    18

*Example: Sports hall*

Daylight also plays an important role in
school buildings and sports halls. Sometimes solutions have to deal with conflicting requirements, such as high daylight
levels, low heat gain and avoidance of
glare.

Burgweinting Primary School's sports hall,
in Regensburg, was developed according to an innovative concept (Figures 17,
18). It has glass facades on all sides, with
glazing that varies according to the direction it faces.

It fulfils the above requirements without
the use of special building elements,
which are generally operable and thus
high maintenance.

The facade facing south is constructed of
photovoltaic insulating glass, absorbing
much of the thermal heat (sun protection)
and, at the same time – despite the large
areas of shading by the photovoltaic
modules – admits sufficient amounts of
daylight into the hall (light transmittance).
To achieve this, the necessary distance
between the individual modules of 20 mm
was determined through light simulation
at the Fraunhofer Institute for Solar
Energy Systems ISE, in Freiburg.

To avoid strong light-dark contrasts on
the interior, the inner panes of glass were
coated with a light-coloured, matt film.
This breaks and scatters light, illuminating
the sports hall without glare. A positive
side effect is that the facade produces
electricity which is fed into the public
power net.

Since the east and west facades would
produce little solar energy, these sides of
the sports hall were not fitted with photovoltaic modules. Translucent, light-scattering insulating glass (Okalux K) was
used to achieve diffuse illumination of the
hall without any glare at all. The north side
is fitted with standard low-E glazing to
provide the maximum delivery of diffuse
light and to offer a view of the sky.

Light simulations confirmed that daylight
levels were sufficient at all points in the
hall, but noticeably higher in its centre
than along the sides. To compensate for
these variations in brightness, the floor in
the peripheral areas (outside the playing
field) was covered in a brighter linoleum
than in the centre.

Good lighting concepts for interior
spaces contribute to well-being. This is
first and foremost achieved by the maximum use of daylight, with its dynamic
qualities and unmistakable properties.
The simulation of daylight by artificial light
can only begin to approach its effects. If
daylight is not available, or available daylight levels are insufficient, it must be supplemented by artificial light. Providing it is
flicker-free, offers the option of controlling
the light level and light colour, and has
good colour rendition, artificial lighting
can play the supporting role to the daylight system. Alternatively, artificial light
could create its own ambience at night
and provide an exciting contrast to the
daylight situation. It cannot, however, not
replace the qualities of daylight.

17, 18  Sports hall at the Burgweinting Primary
School, Regensburg
Architects: Tobias Ruf, Regensburg Architects
Department
Photovoltaic cells are integrated in the insulat-
ing glazing on the south side of the hall. They
produce energy and provide sun protection.
The glass is also coated with a light-scattering
film on the interior.

**Daylight
Characteristics and Basic
Design Principles**

Udo Dietrich

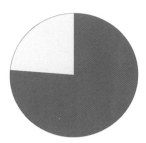

☐ Heating and ventilation
■ Illumination
☐ Hot water

1

## Why use daylight?

Humans take in most sensory information through their eyes. Without light one would not be able to read this text. Light enables spatial perception and orientation. It is light that lets us recognise and distinguish colours. Light makes the world a colourful place!

Colours can be attributed to different moods. Pleasant light can be stimulating, heighten the ability to concentrate and trigger optimistic feelings. Light is essential for our well-being and for comfortable working conditions.

The eye is highly sensitive in assessing light situations. Daylight is generally perceived as more attractive and comfortable than artificial light. There are several reasons for this:

· Light emitted by the sun covers a wide spectrum of frequencies (colours). The blend of these colours makes up white daylight. Artificial light sources cannot exactly reproduce the colour spectrum of the sun. The eye senses this and reacts by tiring more easily.
· Daylight is dynamic. It varies through the seasons and times of day, the position of the sun and cloud cover. Artificial light is static.
· The required amount of artificial light in interior spaces is set at a level required for minimum comfort. Daylight in interior spaces often reaches considerably greater light levels, which is perceived to be more pleasant.
· Daylight is emitted by all sides of the celestial hemisphere and by the sun. Its distribution results in the illumination of the environment. This kind of illumination is comfortable for the eye.

Today's dream home should be first and foremost bright and sunny. Nothing is as unappealing as a gloomy room to live or work in.

A further advantage of daylight is its potential for energy saving. All additional daylight not only means an increase in visual comfort, but also an energy saving in artificial lighting. Potential savings are considerable, especially in office buildings. If the heating standard is up-to-date, the majority of energy will be expended on lighting (Figure 1).

Until recently, this has hardly been recognised. Contemporary energy-efficient architecture no longer means merely improving insulation, but intelligent daylight design.

## How we see

The sky and sun can emit a huge amount of light (high summer, midday and sunshine). This is not a problem for the eye; a high level of light is perceived as pleasant and has an invigorating effect. Looking directly into the sun can be blinding. On the other hand, the eyes also function at dusk; hence a considerably smaller amount of light is entirely sufficient to see perfectly well.

### The Eye

The eye is a sensor that is specially designed for minimal light intensities. If the amount of light increases, the pupil will control how much enters the eye – this prevents the sensor from being overloaded (dazzled).

The eye recognises visible light as only a small section of the sun's spectrum of frequencies. On the surface this seems to be an imperfection, but it is one of nature's ingenious solutions. Nearly half of the sun's total intensity is emitted in a relatively narrow frequency range. This exactly matches the frequency that the eye can receive.

This information is used in the manufacture of solar glass that allows large amounts of solar light to pass through, but 'blocks' the infrared range. This type

1  Proportion of the annual primary energy demand of a typical office building (insulation standard low energy house, no active cooling system, no hot water)
2  Chartres Cathedral, rose window in the north transept, ca. 1240

2

of glazing lets only half of the heat energy into the building in summer (see p. 30).

The eye is able to see spatially. Objects located in different fields of view can be seen because they send light to the eye. These objects are either a light source in their own right, or they reflect light from another source. From each individual viewpoint within the visual range the colour, as well as the brightness of the object looked at, can be recognised and distinguished from the information of a different viewpoint close-by.
Seeing and recognising objects around us is thus achieved through differences in light intensity (luminance L) and colour.

In this context two interesting phenomena can be observed. Spherical light sources with a uniform distribution of light as, for example, the sun, have two particular characteristics:

· Angle projection has the effect of letting the luminous sphere appear like a disc of even intensity.
· Increasing distance makes the light source appear smaller rather than darker. A fixed star in the night sky thus has the same brightness as the sun.

*Glare*
As described above, the eye can perform at low light levels and at very high light levels. This does not necessarily mean that a person can perform a visual task in comfort.
This principle is explained with the help of an example: It is night, the pupil has adapted to a bright object in the field of vision (the source of glare). The field of vision containing the actual visual task, a street sign adjacent to the streetlight, appears too dark for the letters to be legible.

Glare caused by a bright object in the field of vision interferes with the visual task. For the ear a comparable situation would be a loud and interfering noise (traffic) that detracts from the sound of the acoustic task (speech). Glare is a form of visual noise; noise is acoustic glare.

*Physiological glare* verifiably interferes with the visual task. Looking at a bright window (a blue sky is enough) it will be difficult to read information (blackboard/picture) on the wall adjacent to the window. With a person standing in front of a window, one sees a dark silhouette, but not the face. Ceiling luminaires reflected in a computer monitor make it difficult, or even impossible, to read what is on the screen.
Even if the desired information can be read, images with very strong or very weak contrasts can be unpleasant, distracting or interfering. One is not even aware of this *psychological glare* unless the adverse effects are too great, although a reduction in productivity can be detected. The fine adjustment between the actual object examined (monitor/paper) and its surroundings (see p. 10) is essential for the visual task in interior spaces.
For good perception the contrast – the relation of the luminance of nearby objects – should be between three and ten. In the actual work area it should be below three.

A window is reflected in a computer screen. In order to avoid that glare fades the information on the screen the luminance of the reflection must be significantly lower than the self-luminance of the screen: the window needs an anti-glare device reducing the luminance near it. The current limit is set at $L_{max}$ = 400 lm/m² sr. This value cannot be obtained using

Different ranges of the solar spectrum:

| Type of rays | Percent of intensity |
|---|---|
| ultraviolet rays (UV, invisible) | 6% |
| visible light | 48% |
| infrared rays (IR, not visible) | 46% |

Luminance L

The eye can see objects because these send light to the eye. Luminance L [lm/m²sr] is the luminous intensity that is given off at a point on the surface of that object in a certain direction (solid angle, sr). If the eye is facing in this direction, it is the brightness in which the object is seen.
A further commonly used value for luminance is [cd/m²], where [cd = lm/sr] applies.

available anti-glare systems, except if the room is shaded to near darkness. Tests have shown that the limit is set at a value relating to tube monitors of low self-luminance. Modern flat screens are brighter and have anti-reflection properties.

Besides, it is more comfortable for users to open the anti-glare screen and let enough daylight into the room, to have a view out and to maintain contact with the outside world. For this reason luminance values above the limits of the guidelines are accepted. Both cases advocate a readjustment in the threshold set by the German standard, and for anti-glare systems that allow sufficient shading while giving users the opportunity for individual control.

Unlike luminance, illumination is the total available light falling onto a surface. If the spatial distribution of light in a room is relatively even, it can be used to describe the minimum required quantity of light for a particular visual task, and for the stipulation of the uniformity of light distribution. However, it should be noted that, even if the illuminance requirements are met, glare can occur when the light distribution is unfavourable.

Some figures are noted here for a better understanding: At midday on sunny days with a clear sky the illuminance is between 10000 lx (winter) and a maximum of 100000 lx or slightly above (summer). If the sky is overcast the values are considerably lower: 2000 lx in winter to 20000 lx in summer.

Most people feel comfortable at illuminance levels above 2000 lx. This is hardly surprising since this is the quantity of light one will find outdoors during the day, even in bad conditions.

As described above, the eye only requires a fraction of this light to work indoors. Studies have shown that artificial lights are switched on when the illumination drops below 75 lx. This is when colour vision starts to be affected.

The recommendations and regulations of the standards apply higher values. The nominal illuminance is the required illuminance for artificial lighting according to the German standard DIN 5035, depending on the visual task to be performed. For office workplaces, for example, the nominal illuminance is 500 lx, or 300 lx for "daylight-oriented workplaces" (compare pp. 22ff). For work involving more complex visual tasks, that

---

**Illuminance E**

Illuminance E [lm/m² = lx] expresses the total quantity of light from all solid angles on a surface. It is the ratio of the quantity of light falling on a surface and the area that is illuminated.

---

**Nominal illuminance**

The illuminance on a work surface (e.g. a desktop) that must be reached by artificial lighting. The nominal illuminance is stipulated in DIN 5035 (DIN EN 12464) depending on the application. In the integral consideration of artificial lighting and daylight, artificial lights would have to switched on when daylight levels alone are insufficient in reaching the nominal illumination value.

---

**Daylight-oriented workplaces**

According to the wording of DIN 5035 (EN 12464), a workplace in close proximity to a window. A more precise definition can be obtained from the Guidelines for Electric Energy (Leitfaden Elektrische Energie LEE): In daylight-oriented workplaces the daylight autonomy must be at least 70%, meaning that on a minimum of 70% of working hours available daylight levels are sufficient and do not have to be supplemented by artificial lighting. In office space this is equivalent to a daylight factor of approximately 3% (see p. 23).

| Time | 3:00 am | 6:00 am | 9:00 am | noon | 3:00 pm | 6:00 pm | 9:00 pm |
|---|---|---|---|---|---|---|---|
| Position of the sun | NE | E | SE | S | SW | W | NW |
| | | | Altitude of the sun | | | | |
| Winter | – | – | 0 | 15 | 0 | – | – |
| Transitional period | – | 0 | 25 | 40 | 25 | 0 | – |
| Summer | 0 | 20 | 45 | 60 | 45 | 20 | 0 |

3  Daylight hours and position of the sun in Central Europe (values rounded; unit: degrees)

Typical facade in Central or Southern Europe:
The more daylight is available the more closed off
are the facades.
4   Row-housing, Munich;
    Architects: Meck Architekten
5   Residential block, Madrid;
    Architects: Matos-Castillo

of a surgeon or goldsmith for example,
the value is accordingly higher.
The values stipulated by standard DIN
5035 (EN 12464) do not mean that artificial lighting has to be switched on at an
illuminance below 500 lx, but state the
required level of the artificial lighting, i.e.
the size of the artificial lighting system.

**Available daylight in Central Europe**
Solar radiation reaches the earth's surface in two different ways:

- As direct rays from the sun. Direct solar
  radiation provides energy and is easily
  redirected and concentrated (ideal for
  all types of active solar technology). To
  relieve heating systems in winter, sunlight should be let into buildings (passive solar technology). In summer,
  excessive direct daylight entering a
  building will lead to overheating and
  require heat protection measures.
- As diffuse radiation from the sky. Diffuse radiation occurs with a cloud
  cover, partial cloud cover, or when the
  sky is blue. It is considered comfortable
  for general visual tasks and is ideal for
  bringing daylight into interior spaces.

In Central Europe clouds obscure the
sun on 55 % of daylight hours. This means
that the available daylight control systems
which use direct light from the sun are
ineffectual for 55 % of the daylight hours –
precisely when the need for daylight in
interior spaces is greatest because of the
overcast sky.
The daytime hours and the position of the
sun vary significantly in Central Europe
because of its great distance from the
equator. For a first rough estimation the
values (rounded to whole numbers) shown
in the table are sufficient (Figure 3).

A detailed analysis of climatic data in
Central Europe has shown that, because

of the low altitude of the sun, facades facing east and west receive more solar radiation and thus more heat during the summer than those facing south. While the
sun can be easily screened on the south
side when it is at a high elevation (e. g.
using the slats of Venetian blinds), this is
hardly possible with a near horizontal
position of the sun in the west and east
(completely closed blinds turn the heat
protection system into a black-out device
and ventilation blocker).
Therefore, the following applies for office
buildings: offices facing south and north
are preferable to those facing east and
west.

**Daylight apertures in buildings**
To avoid glare, workplaces (especially
those with monitors) should not be exposed to direct sunlight. The resultant
requirements are:

- Every window must have an anti-glare
  device.
- The sky delivers a soft, diffuse light that
  is free of glare at all times during the
  day. It is emitted from all sides – this is
  the light artists obtain in their north-fac-
  ing studios. Hence, the design of daylight apertures is based on the available
  daylight in the sky, and not that of the
  sun.
- Illumination levels of the sky vary greatly
  in Central Europe. Daylight apertures
  are thus dimensioned for dark, overcast
  skies.

The degree to which daylight apertures
can supply light to interior spaces depends on the size, location and characteristics of the opening, and on other
shading obstructions, neighbouring buildings or vegetation.
The absolute minimum is to prevent a
room from appearing gloomy. There
should be sufficient daylight levels in

interior spaces for several hours each day.
A set of very simple planning rules can be
applied here (30°/45° rules) which are further described in the section below. The
rules should always be applied in the
design of housing – even if this is not a
requirement.
The aim for office buildings is to provide
daylight-oriented workplaces. In order to
reduce energy consumption to a conceivable minimum by utilising all available
natural daylight, approximately three
times the amount of light is required,
above the minimum criteria of 'the room
no longer appears gloomy'.

The basic rule of thumb for the design of
daylight apertures is based on the phenomenon that light spreads linearly. Con-
sequently, a workplace in a building has
a good supply of daylight if, from it, one
can see a large section of the light source
sky. This is the case if the path of the ray
of light from the sky to the work surface is
not obscured by neighbouring buildings,
parts of the building one is in, projections,
non-transparent facades or obstructions
on the inside.
If a space is lit from the front only, one will
see the sky if one is close to the window –
the workspace receives much light. But if
one moves into the depth of the space,
the proportion of visible sky decreases,
until finally the view out the window is
reduced to the horizon (and buildings,
trees, etc. on it). This is where the room
starts being gloomy.

The following applies to the design of
room depths: An interior space will be
sufficiently bright if, from this area, the
upper edge of the window is visible at a
minimum vertical angle of 30°.
This means that sufficient amounts of
daylight can penetrate the room to a distance that is equal to twice the height of
the upper edge of the window in that

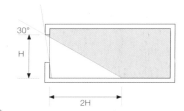

6

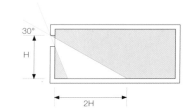

7

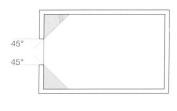

8

room (Figure 6). For example, at a standard ceiling height of 2.7 m, this would be 5.4 m. This equals a maximum overall room depth of 6.0 to 6.5 m including storage and circulation spaces.

The angle of 30° has nothing to do with the position of the sun, but arises from the available light in the sky. The 30° rule thus applies to all directions of the compass and all seasons. High-level windows produce a narrow, dark area below the window parapet caused by shading of the wall in which the window is located (Figure 7).

The 45° rule applies to the lateral distribution of light behind a window: A vertical window admits adequate amounts of lateral light onto areas that lie at an angle of 45° to the left and right of the window (Figure 8).

After projecting the 30° and 45° rules onto a plan, the floor space that is adequately lit can now be easily marked. It is advisable to draw in the furniture. One can tell at a glance if the room can be furnished in a sensible way (Figure 10). Can the main functions be arranged in the space receiving sufficient amounts of light? Can the areas that do not receive sufficient light be allocated a use (cabinets, shelves, TV, circulation area ...)?

Gloomy spaces are caused primarily by vegetation or neighbouring buildings. Shading from opposite objects is a serious problem because it interferes with the direct correlation of sky and floor area, especially for usable floor space in the depth of a room: If the neighbour is located at a great enough distance (or is low enough) for the 30° angle not to be shaded, the path between sky and room depth is unobstructed. The remaining shading of the room can be neglected in a first approximation, i. e. the 30° rule applies (Figures 10–13).

The efficiency of light wells and other horizontal light apertures can be tested using a ruler on a cross-section.

According to the 30° rule, the following applies to skylights: A skylight will provide adequate daylight for those parts of the room that lie beneath an apex angle of 30°. The adequately lit area below the window is equal in width to the height of the room plus the width of the window. This is not much more than the area immediately below the window which receives light from the sky and will be very bright. If the intention of the design is to emphasise a particular area (e.g. reception area), then this can be achieved using a single skylight (Figure 14).

According to the 30° rule, a uniform distribution of light across the entire floor area can be achieved if the distance between the skylights is not greater than the height of the room.

The simple 30°/45° rules are only of limited use. Since they are derived from a constructed two-dimensional cross-section, the resultant light distribution can only be correct if the majority of light actually passes through the window in the constructed direction. This is the case if the windows are of a standard size (a minimum of 30 % ratio of window area[1], each window larger than 1 m²), the room has no external obstructions, or the external obstructions are much wider than the dimensions of the room (e. g. opposite row of buildings).

One example of when the 30°/45° rule cannot be applied is when a single tree partially blocks the window of a room (e. g. the bedroom in Figure 10).

[1] Ratio of window area = Ratio of window area to area of facade

9

Daylight factor

| | >10 % |
| | 9–10 % |
| | 8–9 % |
| | 7–8 % |
| | 6–7 % |
| | 5–6 % |
| | 4–5 % |
| | 3–4 % daylight-oriented |
| | 2–3 % |
| | 1–2 % sufficiently bright |
| | 0.5–1 % |
| | 0–0.5 % gloomy |

1  Bedroom
2  Kitchen
3  Living room
4  Bathroom

10

6   30° rule for a room with lateral light
7   30° rule for a room with a high-level lateral light apertures
8   45° rule shown in plan for lateral light
9   2nd storey, State Bank of Northern Germany, Hanover; Architects: Behnisch & Partner, illumination, workplace in the second row
10  Projection of the 30° and 45° rules onto a floor plan. When adding the furniture, the quality of the room regarding the distribution of daylight can be illustrated.
    Student project, HAW Hamburg, Jasmin Sharif-Neistani, third semester
    The apartment receives sufficient amounts of light from two sides. One of the living spaces is shaded by a conifer, approximately 6 m in height. This room is least inviting during the daytime, and is used – also due to its size – as a bedroom.
    Parapet: 0.85 m (bathroom: 1.40 m)
    Window height: 1.50 m (bathroom: 0.95 m)
11  Simulation of a living space used to demonstrate the 30° rule (Figure 10, 3 living room).
12  Example of a light situation in which the window is obstructed by an object (tree in front of bedroom in Figure 10). Most of the remaining light delivery occurs from the side "behind the tree". This is why the area behind the tree receives the most light. The 30° rule could not be applied in this situation. A computer simulation of the light situation would be necessary (more on computer simulations on p. 25).

11

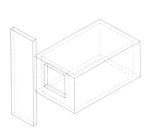

12

Front

Rear – Width (m)

Depth (m)

Front

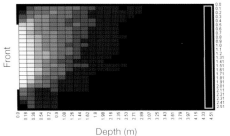

Rear – Width (m)

Depth (m)

13 Shading by neighbouring buildings
14 30° rule for skylights
15 Calculation of areas of sufficient illumination in rooms adjacent to an atrium. The 30° rule can generally not be applied in the lower storeys (see p. 28).

## Daylight quality in interior spaces

The daylight factor D is a value that is well suited to determining the quality of daylight supply at a specific workplace. It describes the illuminance on a work plane inside a room in relation to the outdoor illuminance under an overcast sky.

The daylight factor D is determined solely by the geometry of the space (dimension of room, size and position of windows, shading elements) and the light transmittance properties of the glazing, but not the external illuminance at that particular moment. It is a constant value for each workplace, but varies on a 2-D plane in the room itself.

An example to explain: At an external illuminance of 50 000 lx and a daylight factor D of 1.5 % on the work plane, the illuminance at that point is

$$E = \frac{50\,000\ \text{lx} \times 1.5\,\%}{100\,\%} = 750\ \text{lx}$$

Hence, it is sufficiently bright. If on another work plane D = 0.4 %, the illuminance is only 200 lx, and artificial lights would have to be switched on.

Climatic statistics show the following occurrence of illuminance for our location in Central Europe:

On a day with an overcast sky the external illuminance of

- 2 500 lx is exceeded on 90 % of the daytime hours per year (nearly at all times)
- 5 000 lx is exceeded on 75 % of the daytime hours per year
- 10 000 lx is exceeded on 50 % of the daytime hours per year

For a workplace to reach 300 lx (minimum value for daylight-oriented workplaces

13

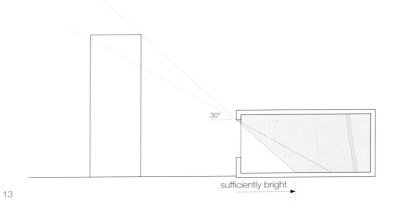

sufficiently bright

14

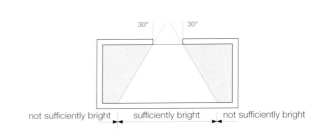

not sufficiently bright | sufficiently bright | not sufficiently bright

15

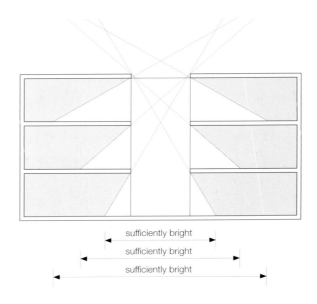

sufficiently bright

sufficiently bright

sufficiently bright

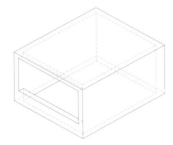

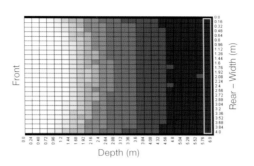

16

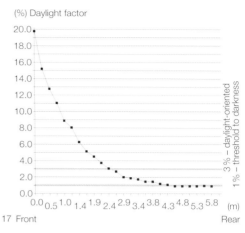

17 Front                                                                 Rear

according to DIN 5035/EN 12464) or at least 75 lx (subjective light threshold for switching on artificial light) the following daylight factor D is required, depending on the outdoor illuminance $E_e$:

| exter. $E_e$ | inter. $E_i$ = 75 lx | inter. $E_i$ = 300 lx |
|---|---|---|
| 2500 lx | D = 3.00% | D = 12% |
| 5000 lx | D = 1.50% | D = 6% |
| 10000 lx | D = 0.75% | D = 3% |

It emerges that the daylight factor of 1%, stipulated in DIN 5034, is the threshold for the absolute minimum. For the majority of working hours the switch-on threshold of 75 lx is achieved, and the room does not appear too dark.

The value of D = 1% can always be obtained for the usable floor space provided the room depth is not too great and there is no shading from nearby buildings.

This interpretation is congruent with the 30°/45° rules. The example on page 21 (Figures 10, 11) shows, by comparison with an exact simulation, the accuracy of these simple rules in meeting the D = 1% threshold.

At a daylight factor D of 3%, 75 lx is reached for 90% of the daytime hours, for 50% of the daytime hours as much as 300 lx is reached. This type of workplace (at D ≥ 3%) can be classified as daylight-oriented (see p. 18).

However, such high illumination levels can only be achieved close to the windows. Illustration 16 shows that in office spaces (free-standing building), a daylight factor of D = 3% can be reached to a depth of approximately equal to the height of the room. That is, assuming a typical ceiling height, just under 3 m room depth.

An even higher daylight factor could, in theory, be reached using larger windows and greater room heights; but this would

not be practicable. The energy demand for artificial lighting would not be significantly reduced, but rather the problems of heat gain in summer exacerbated. Note that initially the energy demand actually drops as the daylight factor increases. A lighting level exceeding the switch-on threshold (300 lx) is then achieved for the majority of working hours. A further increase in daylight factor will not increase energy savings any further. The remaining energy consumption is the result of the time of use at night.

Daylight from the sky is the primary factor determining the amount of light and its distribution in a room.

Other than that, the reflectance of light on (bright) surfaces contributes around 10–20% of light delivery to the centre of the room (i.e. reflectance increases the daylight factor by 1.1–1.2%). If the primary light from the sky is low, reflectance will hardly improve the illumination of a room. It is not really possible to noticeably increase light levels in rooms situated in the depth of a building by using white light wells or atria, for example.

However, the only way to bring daylight into the rear of a large space is by reflection from surrounding surfaces, such as ceilings. This creates a pleasantly uniform distribution of light and reduces stark light-dark contrasts.

$$D = \frac{\text{Illuminance [lx] on an interior work plane (generally horizontal at a height of 0.85 m)}}{\text{Illuminance [lx] on a horizontal plane outdoors under an open, but overcast sky}} \times 100\%$$

D = daylight factor

**Daylight autonomy**

The proportion of annual hours of use in which sufficient amounts of daylight are available and artificial lights do not have to be switched on.

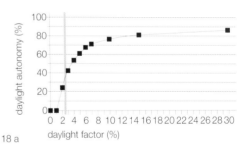

18 a

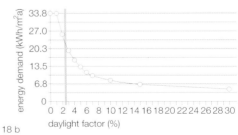

18 b

16  Simulation of a typical office space (4 × 6 × 2.7 m, band of windows at 1.85 m above parapet 0.85 m)
17  Interrelation of daylight factor and room depth
18  a, b Interrelation of daylight factor, energy demand for artificial lighting and daylight autonomy. The grey line demarcates the daylight factor obtained for artificial light in the office space of Figure 16.

19 a  Time of day

b  Time of day

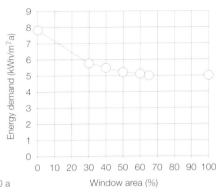

20 a  Window area (%)

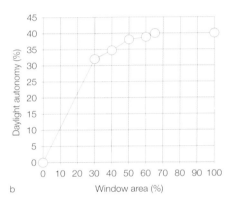

b  Window area (%)

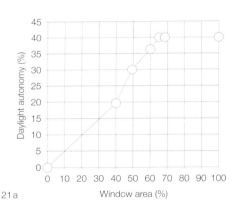

21 a  Window area (%)

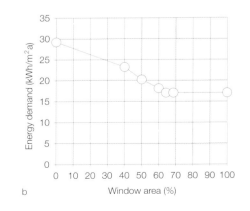

b  Window area (%)

19  Comparison of utilisation profiles of housing (a) and offices (b)
20  a, b  Housing: daylight autonomy and energy demand as a function of window area
21  a, b  Office space: daylight autonomy and energy demand as a function of window area

The quality of daylight at workplaces in office buildings can also be described by the daylight autonomy (Figure 18 a). In daylight-oriented workplaces (D ≥ 3 %) values exceeding 70 % are reached. Since it is not possible to uphold such high standards over the entire floor area, the average value of daylight autonomy at all workplaces should at least be 30 %. Further recommendations for daylight delivery can be found in DIN 5034 – Daylight in Interiors; they are, however, no longer adequate because they were designed to set a minimum standard for daylight levels in dwellings. Further criteria for workplaces are not available, such as energy consumption for artificial light, daylight autonomy and daylight orientation.

*DIN 5034 – Daylight in Interiors*
Recommendations for the daylight factor and a uniform distribution of interior illumination:

- Rooms with lateral light:
  The daylight factor D is calculated for a reference point half way into the room, at a height of 0.85 m and at a distance of 1 m from the lateral wall
- only one vertical window:
  D ≥ 0.75 % (at the less advantageous reference point)
  D ≥ 0.9 %
  (average of both reference points)
- windows on two abutting walls:
  D ≥ 1.0 % (at the less advantageous reference point)
- interior spaces with skylights:
  $D_{avg} ≥ 4 \%$
  (for pleasant lighting, 2 % is considered too dark in rooms with skylights)
  $D_{avg} ≤ 10 \%$
  (to avoid overheating)

Recommendations for an even distribution of interior illumination:

- $D_{min}/D_{max} ≥ 0.67$
- $D_{min}/D_{avg} ≥ 0.5$

## Size and layout of lateral daylight apertures

The following sections examine the optimum number of windows a room should have, and how they should be laid out. There is no pat answer to this question; it depends entirely on the function of the room. In office space, working hours are generally in the daytime (Figure 19 b) and this type of use requires a high nominal illuminance of 500 lux. Hence any change in daylight delivery has a marked effect on the daylight autonomy and energy consumption.

If working hours extend into the (dark) evening hours and the level of nominal illuminance is lower (e. g. living space) a greater supply of daylight will have less effect on the resultant daylight autonomy and energy consumption.
Daylight autonomy for the entire usable floor area of at least 30 % can be assumed to be a criterion of restraint for both uses.

For a typical residential space that has windows in one outer wall, the two diagrams opposite (Figure 20 a, b) illustrate the daylight autonomy obtained depending on the ratio of window area and energy demand for artificial lighting (with the optimum fenestration layout).
The analysis results in the following recommendations regarding the ratio of window area in residential buildings:

- 30 %: Here the desired autonomy of 30 % is already reached. Minimum requirement.
- 40 %: Saturation is almost achieved, sufficiently bright rooms.
- 50 %: The maximum degree of autonomy and energy saving is reached. Optimum value.

22 Information, Communication and Media Centre, Cottbus;
Architects: Herzog & de Meuron
Daylight delivery of lateral light                    22

23

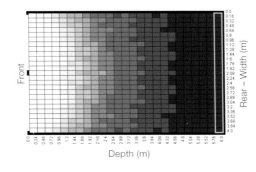

24

Daylight factor

| | |
|---|---|
| >10% | |
| 9–10% | |
| 8–9% | |
| 7–8% | |
| 6–7% | |
| 5–6% | |
| 4–5% | |
| 3–4% | daylight-oriented |
| 2–3% | |
| 1–2% | sufficiently bright |
| 0.5–1% | |
| 0–0.5% | gloomy |

All the lighting scenarios shown here are simulations produced by a computer programme. The room studied is 4 × 6 × 2.7 m in size, the nominal illuminance for the office is 500 lx, and has been assumed at 100 lx for housing (since DIN 5035 does not include residential use).
The daylight factor D on the useable floor space is taken directly from the programme. It is represented in shades of grey, in which the gradations are not linear but follow the visual impression of the eye.

23   Housing with a window area of approximately 40% and the resultant light situation.
Assessment: Sufficiently bright, almost optimum autonomy and energy saving.
24   Office space with a window area of 60% and the resultant light situation.

• Above 50%: A further increase in window area would not improve aspects relating to these two criteria. However, since there are no disadvantages to increasing the window area, up to 65% (above this problems of heat gain may occur in summer) it can be designed to optimise views and the use of passive solar energy.

With respect to daylight, a balcony, according to the 30° rule, reduces the internal area (usable throughout the year) of the apartment below by exactly the area it adds (in temporary use) above. Hence, balconies in apartment blocks should not be larger than the necessary (4 to 5 m², depending on use) and located above enclosed areas of the apartment below.

For typical office space that has windows in the facade, the two diagrams opposite (Figure 21 a, b) illustrate the daylight autonomy attained, depending on the ratio of window area and energy demand for artificial lighting (with the optimum fenestration layout). Analysis results in the following recommendations regarding the ratio of window area:

• 50%: below this the desired autonomy of 30% is not reached. Minimum requirement.
• 60%: saturation is almost reached, sufficiently bright rooms.
• 65%: the maximum degree of autonomy and energy saving is reached. Optimum value.
• Above 65%: A further increase in window area would not be advantageous in respect of these two criteria.

A 65% window area is the threshold beyond which office space (depending on the degree of mechanisation, illumination, type of glazing and protection

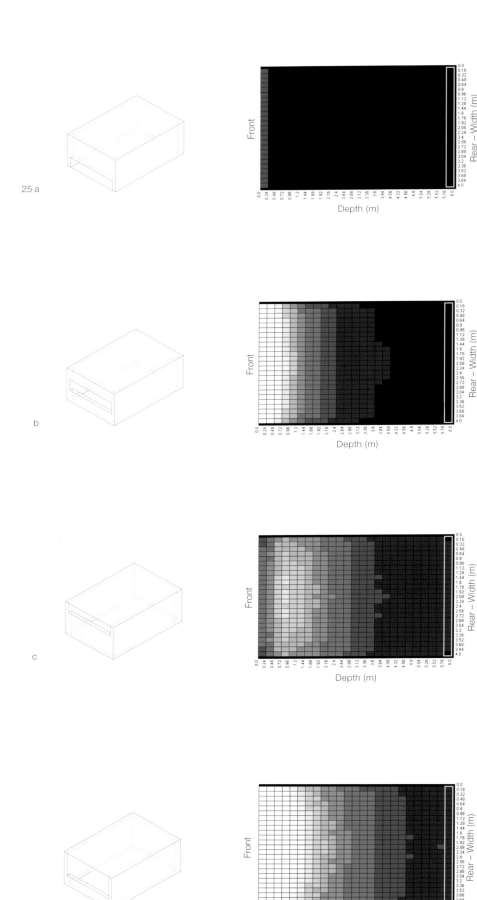

25 a

b

c

d

against overheating) cannot effectively offset heat gain in summer by using passive measures.

Further binding requirements for workrooms, depending on their size, are stipulated in the Workplace Directive. This states the minimum requirement for the glazed area of all windows in a room:

- At a room height of 3.50 m and a usable floor area of 50 m² this should be more than 30 % of the area of the facade.
- In larger rooms it should be more than 10 % of the usable floor space.

With a fixed ratio of window area, the distribution of light in a room, and thus the daylight autonomy, varies greatly according to the position of the apertures (see Figure 25 a–d). High, narrow windows with non-transparent areas between them result in better daylight supply than a continuous window band of the same dimensions at mid-height.

A window at parapet level does not provide light in the depth of the room.

A window of equal dimensions at midheight provides much light to the front of the room but does not deliver sufficient light to the rear. The area close to the window is often too bright (glare).

A high-level window, if possible without lintel and extending to the ceiling, provides the best illumination. The distribution of light is even and light penetrates the depth of the room.

Illustration 25 d shows the standard solution for office space which has a 60 % ratio of window area in the upper two thirds of the facade. An adequate amount of daylight is delivered to the depth of the room; close to the facade the high illumination levels may cause glare.

With a favourable fenestration layout, a 50% ratio of window area is sufficient for the best results in terms of autonomy and economy of energy (with few problems regarding heat gain in summer, Figure 27). The upper third of the facade is entirely glazed (optimum supply of daylight in the depth of the room), the middle third is partially glazed (about half, view out).

Additionally, this layout leaves 50 % of the facade free for other uses, such as separate ventilation apertures or active solar technology.

The most important comfort criterion is the view out. The eye's main field of view is shaped something like a flattened funnel. In this field the line of vision should

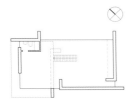

26 a

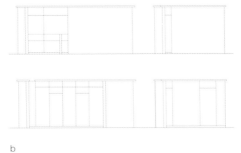

b

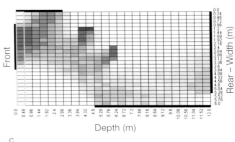

c

27

meet a transparent window area. The projection to the facade of a seated person's field of view, at a typical workplace several metres into the room, directs recommendations for the size of windows required for a view (DIN 5034):

· Lower edge of glazing ≤ 0.90 m above floor level
· Upper edge of glazing ≥ 2.20 m above floor level (the resultant minimum height of glazing is 1.30 m, the overall height of the window is 1.30 m plus the top and bottom frames)
· Width of glazing of a window ≥ 1.0 m, in rooms of more than 5 m depth ≥ 1.15 m
· Width of glazing of all the windows in the facade of the room ≥ 55 % of the width of the room.

Irrespective that the objective may be to achieve the best illumination with light from all sides, additional, smaller apertures can contribute to the (light) ambience of a space and provide opportunities for views to the outside (Figure 26 a–c). However, it should be noted that two large windows arranged on abutting walls, or on opposite sides of the room, can cause unpleasant shadows, as well as glare.

Lighting large interior spaces, such as in schools or sports halls, requires special treatment. These spaces are generally of great depth. To obtain adequate, evenly distributed light, ideally without causing glare, the light apertures must be either on two opposite walls or in the roof. The daylight factor should be at least 3 % for the entire usable floor area and it should be distributed evenly.

This is easy to achieve up to a 3 to 1 ratio of width to height and by arranging windows on opposite walls. These spaces may be stacked in storeys on top of one

another. It is recommended to use two different windows; one large main window with clear glazing (in classrooms on the wall to the left of the main direction of view), and an additional smaller band of windows (possibly scattering diffuse light) at the top of the opposite wall. This will limit disturbing shadows cast only to one side (good visual comfort, but not for left-handed people). The additional window significantly increases the area that receives daylight (Figure 29).

If it is possible to employ skylights, the usable floor area directly beneath them can be supplied with sufficient daylight. The openings in the roof can be either horizontal or vertical. To obtain a uniform distribution of light they should be spaced at a distance equivalent to the height of the room (30° rule, p. 20). Depending on the type of glazing used, a mere 7 to 15 % of the roof area is required to achieve a daylight factor of at least 4 %. Larger areas of glazing would, without shading, lead to heat gain.
In stepped roofscapes or sawtooth sections, light apertures can be integrated in the vertical surfaces. Depending on the layout, a glazed area of at least one third to half of the usable floor area beneath is required to light the space, often in combination with vertical glazing at user level (Figure 31).

Since providing views out is not required by skylights, heat gain and light incidence are easily controlled with external shading devices, or measures in the space between the panes of double glazing that convert direct sunlight into diffuse light (see Chapter "Daylight Control"). Generally, it should be noted that admitting diffuse light also admits solar heat. Hence, over-dimensioned glazed areas that are exposed to direct sunlight should be avoided.

25  Example of how the height of a window affects the distribution of daylight in an interior space:
     a  low window (between 0 to 0.9 m high)
     b  mid-level window (between 0.9 to 1.8 m high)
     c  high window (between 2.8 to 2.7 m high)
     d  mid-level and high window (standard layout)
26  a, b  Outline proposal for an artist's studio. In addition to the main fenestration in the northeast and the southwest/northwest corner, the light ambiance is accentuated by narrow light slits.
     c  The simulation shows the light situation in plan.
        Student project HAW Hamburg, Lydia Ax and Andrea König, fourth semester.
27  In terms of lighting, the optimum layout of fenestration in office buildings (50 % window area).

28 a         b

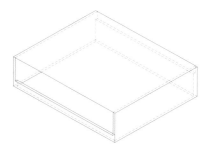

Front    Rear – Width (m)

Depth (m)

29

28   a, b Classroom, special-needs school, Freising,
      Architect: Eberhardt Schunk. Good illumination
      through main glazing and band of high-level
      windows on opposite side.
29   Classroom with a ratio of room depth to height of
      3:1; the transparent main area of glazing and ad-
      ditional (translucent) glazing on the opposite side
      provide good illumination of the entire area.
30   Otto-Locher Sports Hall, Rottenburg; Architects:
      Ackermann and Raff. Uniform illumination
      through glazing integrated into the roof.
31   Large hall with a ratio of room depth to height
      6:1; the roofscape with integrated vertical glazing
      provides good illumination for the entire area.
      Anti-glare devices and shading measures are
      necessary on the side facing the sun.

### Adverse effects of external shading by buildings

Daylight delivery to interior spaces can be adversely affected by existing conditions that are not actually related to the fenestration. These built external elements that cause shading may be buildings located opposite, buildings sited at right angles to the space in question, and also horizontally – projecting building elements in front of or above the daylight opening of the room.

Shading from opposite buildings reduces available light, especially farther from the facade (Figure 32 a, b, c). Taking the ratio of distance d to height h of the neighbouring building, the following rule of thumb can be applied:

- d : h > 2.7 no adverse effect
- d : h > 2.0 slight adverse effect
- d : h > 1.0 high adverse effect
- d : h < 1.0 severe adverse effect

The same rules apply for (office) space facing onto a courtyard or an atrium. In administrative buildings, the offices located adjacent to an atrium, at least on the lower levels of the building, are generally too dark (also see p. 22). Hence, uses that require less daylight (circulation spaces, conference rooms, etc.) should be located here; otherwise the opening of the atrium towards the top should be widened.

Lateral shading by parts of the (L-shaped) building at hand, or by nearby buildings, removes a lot of light, but only in the section of the room nearest windows; the illumination at the back of the room is hardly affected.

As a rule of thumb, in the corner of such an L-shaped building the first 8 to 10 m receive less light (Figure 34 a, b, c) and so secondary functions, such as stairs,

toilets, kitchens, print rooms, etc., are best located here.

In addition fixed, horizontal slats at windows result in a considerable loss of light, especially on dull days.

Shading devices should be sufficiently flexible to be completely retracted.

An exception is the use of fixed louvres or overhangs with a shading angle of 35° on the south-facing facades of office buildings. The exact angle is produced when the ratio of the width of lamella to the distance between slats, or to the projection, is 0.7. This ensures that the shadow covers the entire window area during high summer – no further shading devices at window level are needed to prevent direct sunlight from entering the room. Additional protection against solar gain is not really necessary. The window remains unobstructed, offering outside views, and it can be opened for ventilation. In office buildings, extra anti-glare measures are required in seasons when the sun is low in the sky. These can be attached on the inside of the window. Fixed horizontal building elements result in considerable daylight reduction, and artificial lights are switched on more often. Therefore, this alternative is only recommended for south-facing buildings. Even with buildings facing southeast and southwest, the shading angle would have to be 45° because of the lower altitude of the sun – the resultant loss of daylight would be too great.

30

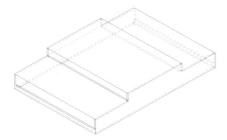

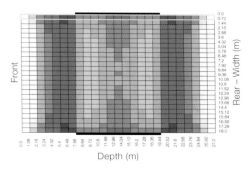

31

## Daylight control

A large, clear area of glazing will transmit as much light as possible, offer the best view and admit the maximum amount of daylight.

However, the resulting light condition is not necessarily the best for the performance of the (visual) task at hand. A secondary device is required controlling the incidence of light. It is generally installed at window level. The functions are diverse and partly contradictory:

- screen direct sunlight (anti-glare),
- reduce the brightness of the sky (also anti-glare, mainly for computer workstations),
- admit sufficient daylight when the system is shut and distribute it pleasantly (energy saving, comfort),
- maintain an unobstructed view, even when the device is shut,
- avoid excessive heat gain during summer (overheating protection),
- permit (natural) ventilation, even when the device is shut,
- permit control of all conceivable exterior conditions and all possible work situations on the inside.

The 'ideal' shading that would fulfil the above criteria does not exist in the current standard of available technology. However, there are devices that fulfil most of the desired functions and come close to offering a solution.

To select the right solution for an actual building project further criteria are relevant:

How can the system be assessed with regard to straightforwardness (manufacture, operation, formal), sustainability and suitability (in terms of utilisation of a building, architectural expression, overall budget)? And finally: does it serve the purpose of architecture in that it creates pleasant spaces for people?

*Active principles*

Systems for directing daylight are elements that interfere with the linear passage of light as it passes through openings in the facade. They reduce, redirect, bundle, scatter or dim light, or single sections of the spectrum (Figure 35 a–d). Different systems can operate on one or several active principles at the same time; they can be used either individually or in combination, as part of a complex facade system that fulfils all functions of the building skin, or in a modular fashion. Furthermore, they are also dissimilar in the part of the building to which they are applied (the facade/windows or roofs/skylights) or in the type of light they use (direct sunlight or diffuse light from the sky) in being either flexible or static, or in their location in front of, behind, or in-between the glazing layers.

In terms of thermal technology, it is of course best to have the external shading device as far away from the glazing as possible. Solar rays are intercepted "at the front", and shading devices that heat up in the sun (40 °C is not uncommon) are cooled right away in the external air, so that little thermal radiation will enter the room. Exterior shading devices are associated with (solvable) problems of rot and wind damage.

If the side of the device facing the sun has a metal coating, solar radiation is efficiently reflected in the visible spectrum as well as in the infrared range. The system itself is less susceptible to heat gain and can, while set at the correct angle, direct daylight far into the depth of a room. Because even the slightest amount of soiling reduces the effect, such a device must be placed either in the cavity between layers of glazing, between the glazing of a double facade or double windows, or on the inside of the fenestration.

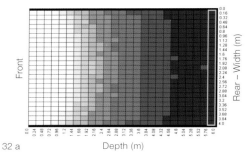

32 a     Depth (m)

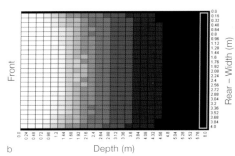

b     Depth (m)

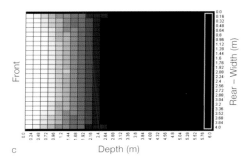

c     Depth (m)

Double glazing of different values for solar factor sf and light transmittance τ

| | | |
|---|---|---|
| Low-E glazing | sf = 0.60 | τ = 0.70 |
| Solar glazing (coloured) | sf = 0.21 | τ = 0.25 |
| Solar glazing (uncoloured) | sf = 0.33 | τ = 0.66 |

33

32 Light simulation for an office space with different shading scenarios caused by buildings.
   a   Free-standing building
   b   Distance to height ratio of the building opposite is 2:1
   c   Distance to height ratio of the building opposite is 1:1
34 a, b, c  Effect of an 'L-shaped' obstruction on available light. The diagram on the left shows the first room (located in the corner) to have a considerable loss of illumination, the second room a just perceptible loss, and the third hardly any at all. The diagram on the right shows the situation without shading.
35 Active principles of daylight control

The position of the shading device is determined by its heat-protection function. The position is of no consequence to daylight.

The commonly available products are briefly described below. For systems that primarily serve purposes of daylight optimisation, rather than shading, see section "Daylight control" (p. 42ff).

*Solar glazing*
The aim of applying different coatings to the panes of glass is to keep the transmission of solar radiation to a minimum, or, in other words, to keep the solar factor (total energy transmittance g) as low as possible. Effective daylight delivery is only possible at high light transmittance τ. However, coated glass has a more or less adverse effect on light transmittance, as is its colour neutrality (Figure 33).

Colour-neutral solar glazing does not entail a significant loss of daylight and its effect is negligible on user comfort (selectivity, the ratio of light transmission to the total energy transmittance is almost 2.0). In most cases a simple, internal shading device or overheating protection is sufficient; the minimum requirement for office

workplaces is an anti-glare device. In buildings with generously proportioned window areas, the use of colour-neutral solar glazing can be a sensible alternative to low-E glazing in combination with external protection against overheating. The low light transmittance of glazing that is not colour-neutral (gold, silver ...) necessitates more than 100 working hours per annum in which artificial lights must be switched as it is too dark at the workplaces.

*Printed glazing*
Another option is to print on sections of the pane of glass using the screen print technique (grid, stripes, etc.) to reduce the incidence of daylight. It is primarily used in situations where obstruction of the view out does not matter (skylights, large areas of glazing) or where the view is intentionally blocked.

*Dimmable glazing*
Set off by a controllable impulse (either electric, thermal, or other impulses) the pane of glass darkens or turns cloudy, and thus reduces the amount of radiation passing through it. Dimmable glazing reduces solar radiation to the same extent as an external blind and its thermal

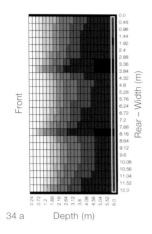

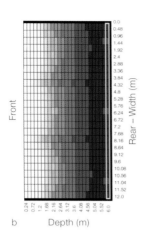

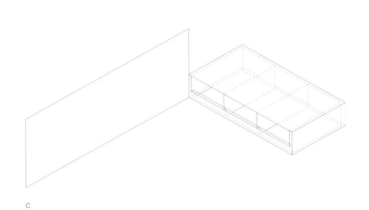

34 a     Depth (m)        b     Depth (m)        c

protection properties during summer are equally efficient.

However, it may react sluggishly to controls (approximately 30 minutes) and the degree of dimming can, in some cases, not be controlled. If the glazing is the type that turns cloudy instead of dark, the view out is lost. The sun shining into the room can still lead to glare. Furthermore, the glazing in its switched off "clear" state, does not have the same light transmittance properties as ordinary low-E glazing and artificial light has to be turned on sooner (Figure 36 a–c). This should all be considered when using dimmable glazing in office buildings. At the current level of development, dimmable glazing is suitable for halls with large glazed areas – especially for inclined or irregularly shaped glazed areas where the sitting and fitting of conventional devices would be difficult.

*Blinds and awnings*
Blinds and awnings work according to a smart principle: radiation from the sun is screened while light from the sky is let in. Blinds with adjustable horizontal slats can direct light far into a room. A metallic, strongly reflective coating makes these highly efficient, but they need to be installed where they are protected from dirt: on the inside.
The user benefits from blinds in the comfortable "cut-off" position that screens the sun while letting in light from the sky between the slats and permitting views out. However, the situation is not satisfactory when the sun is low in the sky (winter/west facade): the slats then have to be shut all the way. Perforating the slats can help. If the proportion of holes is 5 %, glare from the sun is prevented while views out are still possible.
To counteract the unintended darkening of a room when the slats are shut com-

pletely, separate control of the upper third of the slats is possible. More daylight can enter the room through this section (Figures 37, 39).
The slats can be installed on the outside or in the space between the panes of glass (also see section "Active principles").
Awnings screen direct sunlight by casting a shadow in the area in front of a window. Views are possible from under the awnings. Here, too, the sun at low altitude is a problem.

*Solar-film rolling blinds and screens*
Rolling blinds, made of translucent film with a metallic coating, or screens of perforated fabric are placed directly in front of the window. Both reduce solar radiation and the light from the sky.
The disadvantage is that the sun shining through the shading device can still cause glare so that additional anti-glare devices may be necessary.
Advantages of these systems are unobstructed views, easy installation (protected from the weather behind at least one layer of glazing) and low maintenance.
Solar-film rolling blinds are not typically drawn from top to bottom, but from bottom to top. A workplace near the window can be shaded while the upper sections remain open to provide the necessary illumination (Figures 38, 39).

*Prisms*
Prisms are generally made of plastic and integrated into double glazing.

*Microsheds*
Light-control glass with acrylic profiles which have a metallic coating and are integrated in the space between panes of double glazing. They cut off direct sunlight while taking diffuse light from the sky to the interior.

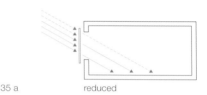

35 a     reduced

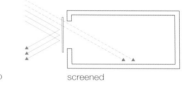

b     screened

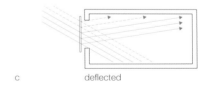

c     deflected

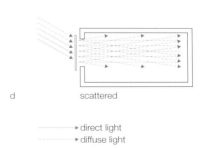

d     scattered

→ direct light
→ diffuse light

31

36 a

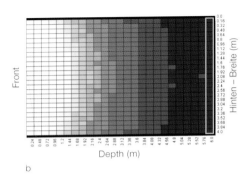

b

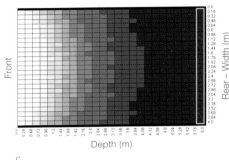

c

*Laser-Cut Panels (LCP)*
Laser-contoured acrylic glass in the cavity of double glazing that directs light by means of total reflection.

*Fixed horizontal profiles*
Rigid profiles, generally in the cavity of double glazing, that direct light by means of reflection (metal profiles) or total reflection (acrylic profiles).

*Holographic Optical Elements (HOE)*
These can integrate almost all optical features into a special transparent film that is embedded in the glazing.

*Heliostats*
Heliostats collect sunlight and direct it into the building's core via metallised pipes/light conducting cables.

*Anidolic systems*
Anidolic (non-imaging) systems direct diffuse light into a space and thereby concentrate its effect.

**Design example: Office space**
The example of the standard office space, as previously shown, (4 × 6 × 2.7 m, height of window band 1.85 m above parapet level of 0.85 m) is employed to assess the practical application of the numerous available systems for directing daylight (shading devices and daylight control).

*Analysis of the light situation*
The first thing that needs to be established is the type of light required by the user. Must a constant level be maintained in a room void of brighter objects, as would be required for computer workstations? Or should it be bright? Is the play of sun specks an option or even wanted? Does the light really have to be white, or is a modest play of colours considered pleasant?

What light situation is created by a daylight system when the sun shines – when it is high in the sky (summer, south side), low (winter, south side/summer, east and west sides) or shining across the facade?
What light situation is created by a daylight system when the sky is overcast? As mentioned previously, this is the most common situation in Central Europe, and thus an important aspect in the assessment.

*Analysis of daylight autonomy*
The analysis should begin by setting threshold values on the criteria for daylight autonomy and energy demand. The maximum possible daylight autonomy can be established if one assumes that to supply a space with as much daylight as possible is the sole concern. Aspects controlling the amount of light (and thereby reducing the autonomy), anti-glare devices and heat protection are disregarded. The relevant model for this situation would be a space with clear glazing and without any shading devices at all. The maximum possible daylight autonomy is determined by the geometry of a space, the position and size of the fenestration, orientation, usage (nominal illumination and time of use) and the furnishing of the room (location of workplaces).
For a regular office space the daylight autonomy throughout the year is just above 40%. This remarkably high value is reduced when calculated for all seasons:

- Summer: high autonomy, sufficient daylight is available for most working hours.
- Spring/autumn: medium autonomy, generally sufficient daylight is available on 30 to 40% of working hours.
- Winter: low autonomy, work is done almost exclusively in artificial light.

For most of the year the available light will be sufficient. But the winter months' short, generally overcast days provide only a few hours of sufficient daylight. Obviously, any additional shading or daylight system at the window will reduce the amount of light entering a room. A possible advantage could be that the reduced amount of light is distributed more evenly. Experience has shown that on overcast days the light situation with the use of a daylight system is no worse than when using clear glazing.

To avoid office space having to be artificially lit throughout the winter months, the following rule should be applied: Shading and daylight control systems should be completely retractable. Rigid systems are only acceptable if the resultant light situation in the interior on overcast days is not worse than that without the system.

*Analysis of energy demand*

The maximum energy demand is reached with the "lights on" option for the duration of the entire time of use (typical of many open plan offices of the 1970s). The minimum energy demand occurs at the maximum daylight autonomy (i.e. without a shading system). It is generally greater than zero (just as the maximum daylight autonomy is less than 100%) because (in winter) it is dark outside for some of the working hours.

For the office space examined, the following exemplary threshold values apply:

- Maximum energy demand ("lights on") 29 kWh/m²a
- Minimum energy demand (no shading system) 17 kWh/m²a

*Assessment*

The assessment of different systems for controlling daylight can be carried out relatively easily when comparing these to a good, established system.

Venetian blinds, installed on the outside, with perforated slats that can be operated independently in the upper third of the window, are used as a reference in this instance.

The annual balance shows that, in comparison to the ideal situation of having "no shading device" at all, the number of working hours in which artificial light is required is reduced by approximately 30%. Daylight autonomy is just above 30%, a value that is acceptable. The energy demand has increased by 5 kWh/m² as compared to the possible minimum. These figures have been taken from a detailed study of an administration building, conducted by the author. Since the result is not only influenced by the shading device used, but also by the geometry of the space, its orientation and nominal illuminance, exact figures are not stated as they cannot be generalised. A first assessment should now compare a new shading device with these figures. In a more detailed analysis of the deficit in autonomy, three scenarios can be identified:

- Overcast sky. Ideally, the shading device is completely retracted. No detrimental effects are expected.
- Sunshine directly onto the facade. The shading system would have to be shut. Almost all cases of loss of autonomy are the direct result of this situation. How much daylight will penetrate the room through a closed device?
- Sunshine, but the sun is behind the facade. Here too, the shading device can be retracted (except for its possible use as overheating protection). No detrimental effects are expected.

A secondary, and in part subjective assessment includes other criteria, such as the distribution of light, retaining a

36 Dimmable glazing in office space.
Poor light transmittance properties of dimmable glazing in its clear state leads to a reduction in daylight autonomy below the recommended minimum value of 30%. At 2500 hours of use per annum, artificial lights would have to be switched on for more than 375 hours.
 a Reference room for office space with a window area of 65%, assumed hours of use per annum 2500 h
 b Two panes of low-E glass, light transmittance 75%, daylight autonomy 43% (on 1075 h sufficient daylight), energy demand 16.4 kWh/m²a
 c Dimmable glazing in its clear state, light transmittance 50%, daylight autonomy 28% (on 700 h sufficient daylight), energy demand 20.6 kWh/m²a
37 Office building, Munich; Architect: von Seidlein. Venetian blinds with separate setting in the upper third.

37

38

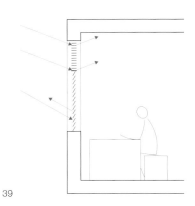

39

38  Solar-film rolling blinds, drawn from the bottom to the top
39  The detailed examination of a window has shown that it can be divided into zones of different functions: The upper third (above a height of 2 m approximately) is for admitting daylight since it is this section of a window that provides the best illumination, especially in the depth of a room. The function of the two lower thirds (from the parapet to a height of 2 m) is to provide a view. This separation of functions allows for the installation of devices for the control of daylight:
In case of glare the lower third is closed. The work area of a person in that room is shaded. To maintain a view out, perforated film or slats can be used.
The upper section can remain open to let in daylight and to provide a sightline to the sky. A light-deflection system could also be installed. In case of overheating the upper part of the window is closed as well.
There are two types of devices based on this principle:
• Venetian blinds with separate controls for slats in the upper third.
• Solar-film rolling blinds/screens that are not, as usual drawn from top to bottom, but from the bottom to the top.

view, and the possibility of ventilating the room while the shading device or daylight system is in use.
The study found that none of the three scenarios had any convincing advantages over the reference scenario. However, the study examined one isolated room only, and not a whole building with numerous rooms of varying proportions, uses and orientations, for which an overall solution would have to be developed.

**Daylight and building shape**
The analysis of a typical residential building shows that, in spite of the current high standard of insulation, just over 50% of fossil fuel consumption is used for heating (Figure 40). Although the energy consumption for hot water and artificial light is considerable, the following principles apply to designing for low energy demand:

• The shape of the insulating building skin should be compact (a small "area/volume ratio")
• All of the usable floor area should receive sufficient amounts of daylight (daylight factor ≥ 1%).

Optimum-energy residential buildings will, in future, also be designed as compact building volumes. Sufficient illumination levels are achieved using the typical building depths of 12 to 15 m.
The analysis of a typical office building with high insulation standards has led to fundamentally different results (Figure 41). Due to a more intense utilisation and longer usage hours, but most of all because of the higher nominal illumination, most of the fossil fuel is required for electricity to power artificial lighting.
To achieve the lowest possible energy demand, the following design rules should be applied:

• All usable floor space should receive sufficient daylight (daylight factor D ≥ 1%, daylight autonomy ≥ 30%),
• the highest possible proportion of the usable floor space should be daylight-oriented (D ≥ 3%, see p. 18).

The office building of the future will thus be a rather slender, narrow, light-flooded volume. Such buildings could be very elegant, may open up to the environment and communicate with their surroundings.

**The facade as a complex system**
The function of a facade is not restricted to protecting buildings form the weather, noise and burglary, but also to allow exchange and communication between the interior and exterior. Influences reducing comfort are kept out while influences increasing comfort should be allowed in, according to the wishes of the user (fresh air, daylight sunshine, views, communication, birdsong ...).
The sought-after "communicative" aspects of a facade can be listed as follows:

• View: a person is generally seated a few metres behind the facade. The main field of view towards the facade extends at a height of 0.9 m to 2.2 m and is at least 1 m wide (compare page 27). This defines the position and size of clear glazing that is required for a view.
• Communication with the outside world: to maintain contact with the outside and to admit into the room a specific atmosphere ("spring has arrived"), the window that opens to the inside must be at least the size and position of the upper body of a standing person. Its position is identical to the requirements for a 'view'. The size of the window can be limited by subdividing the fenestration at a height of 0.9 to 2.0 m.

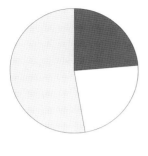

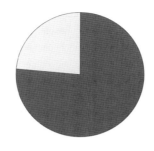

40
☐ Heating and ventilation
■ Lighting
☐ Hot water

41
☐ Heating and ventilation
■ Lighting
☐ Hot water

40 Proportion of the annual primary energy demand of a typical residential building (insulation standard low energy house, no active cooling system)
41 Proportion of the annual primary energy demand of a typical office building (insulation standard low energy house, no active cooling system, no hot water)

• Supply of daylight: High-level windows provide a great deal of light that is distributed evenly across the space (compare p. 26). The upper third (above the part of the window that can be opened) of the facade should be allocated this function. Additional elements which deflect light can be incorporated.
• Natural draught-free ventilation: The room can be aired by opening the window. On days with inclement weather this may lead to draughty conditions. In such cases it is preferable to use the aperture in the upper third of the facade for ventilation purposes.

A possible alternative is to have an additional, separate ventilation aperture. To ventilate a space via the facade, the ventilation aperture must be 4 % of the floor area. This is equivalent to approximately 10 % of the facade in typically dimensioned spaces (ratio of room height to room depth 1 to 2.5). According to the thermal principle, the best ventilation aperture would be narrow and the same height as the room.
If in office buildings the ventilation apertures are burglar-proof as well as weather-proof, they may be left open outside working hours; this contributes to the cooling of building components at night in summer.

The elements of the facade listed above follow the principle of function separation. Additional elements, such as anti-glare or shading devices and daylight control systems, possibly even systems for the active utilisation of solar energy (photovoltaic) are assembled into a catalogue of single modules that – just like in a mosaic – must be combined to form a meaningful whole.
The principle of disentanglement of the facade, a complex system shaped by often conflicting functions, must be

applied before the optimisation process can begin.

Illustrated below are examples of two office buildings with efficient system facades that were developed according to the described method.

*Fraunhofer Institute for Solar Energy
Systems ISE in Freiburg*

Laboratories, workshops and offices at
the ISE are all grouped together in one
new building that was designed and created on the premise of a high quality
workplace with good functionality at low
energy consumption levels.

At concept stage, the architects' design
alternatives were tested with the help of
engineers who examined and assessed
aspects of thermal insulation, anti-glare
protection, lighting and ventilation.

The implemented design has a sawtooth
roof offering ideal preconditions for energy
optimisation. Office space, preferably not
air-conditioned, is located on the south
side of the building wing, the associated
laboratories that require air-conditioning
are on the north side. South-facing offices avoid the uncomfortable effects of
the sun at low altitudes on east and west
facades throughout the year (glare or
lack of views due to shading and anti-
glare devices being closed for much of
the time).

The siting of laboratories and office space
on one level results in a ceiling height of
3.3 m which, in combination with a room
depth of 5 m only, facilitates good utilisation of daylight. The office facade is
divided into four segments: parapet, window, anti-glare panel and skylight. The
skylight, set flush in the ceiling, is particularly effective in delivering daylight to the
depth of the space, and the window in
delivery of daylight to desks (illumination
and view). External louvres (supplemented
by an internal anti-glare blind), with two
independent controls, offer sun protection
and allow light to enter through the top
segment deep into the space. The remaining 50 % of the facade is not glazed
but designed as closed panels to prevent heat gain during the summer. Photovoltaic modules may be mounted on the
parapet.

The concept for artificial lighting in the
office space is attuned to the large
amounts of available daylight: The basic
illumination is obtained from standard
luminaires giving off indirect lighting.
They work with a centrally controlled electric circuit responding to daylight levels;
work places are lit by manually controlled
desk luminaires which, in areas of low
daylight levels, are fitted with a switch
module responding to presence. Light
simulations during the design stage had
shown that the cost of a light control system responding to daylight levels is only
cost-effective in areas of poor daylight
availability.

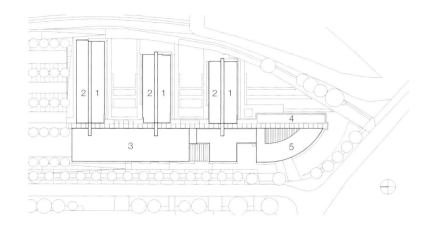

42

43

1 Office space
2 Laboratory
3 Plant, workshops
4 Administration
5 Central services, entrance

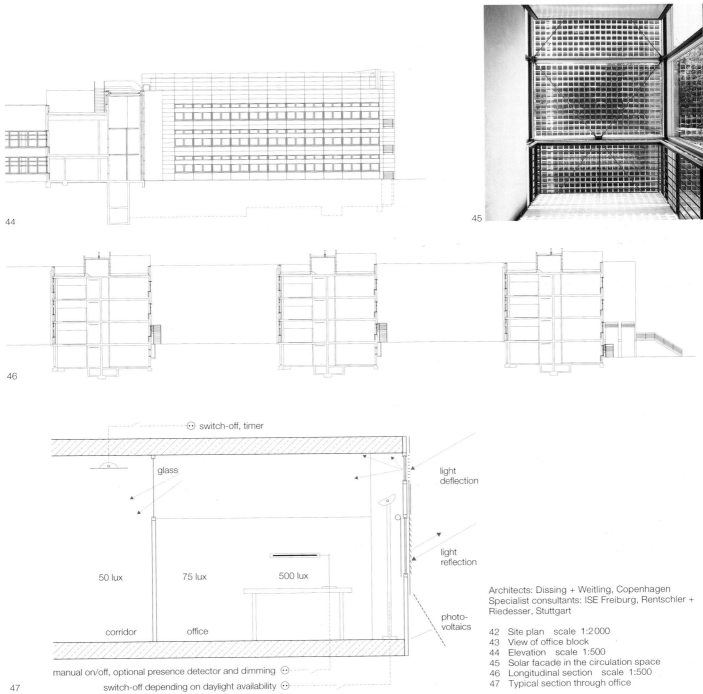

44

45

46

47

switch-off, timer

glass

light
deflection

light
reflection

50 lux    75 lux    500 lux

photo-
voltaics

corridor    office

manual on/off, optional presence detector and dimming

switch-off depending on daylight availability

Architects: Dissing + Weitling, Copenhagen
Specialist consultants: ISE Freiburg, Rentschler +
Riedesser, Stuttgart

42 Site plan   scale 1:2000
43 View of office block
44 Elevation   scale 1:500
45 Solar facade in the circulation space
46 Longitudinal section   scale 1:500
47 Typical section through office

*Administration building in Wiesbaden*
The office building for the Supplementary Pension Fund is located near Wiesbaden's main railway station. The four narrow building volumes are oriented to maintain the east-westerly air current that is important to the city's climate. Double transverse access corridors, extending in a north-south direction, link the five buildings. Two vertical access cores are located within each building at the point of intersection with the corridor axes. They are accessible from the street so that each section can be used and rented independently.

The office blocks are in-situ reinforced concrete frame structures. Their flat roofs are dimensioned to avoid the use of beams. The floor area can accommodate all types of layouts, individual offices, group offices and combination offices, or open plan.

The building is characterised by an intelligent facade including a sophisticated daylight control system, flexible ventilation, as well as by several energy features. The appearance of the south facade is determined by shovel-shaped sun protection and light deflection panels made of aluminium (see p. 40). The modules are automatically moved to deflect direct sun-

48

light, making sure that the lighting of the office space is compatible with EDP workplaces at all times. The external appearance of the building constantly changes as the positions of the panels are altered in response to the weather. Light deflection panels were also employed on the north sides of the buildings, but these are immobile.

Behind the panels is a post and beam facade with insulated triple glazing. In conjunction with the adjustable building component heating and cooling system, comfortable indoor temperatures are achieved at low energy consumption.

Wooden ventilation sashes that can be adjusted manually are incorporated in the sides of the facade sections. Fresh air that can be preheated by built-in convectors is directed into the room via integrated plastic louvres. The interior space is ventilated and a pleasant temperature maintained, even when the sashes are shut. The system is flexible and user-friendly.

Architects: Herzog + Partner, Munich
Energy concept: Kaiser Consult, Hausladen, Oesterle, DS-Plan
Lighting design: Bartenbach Lichtlabor

49

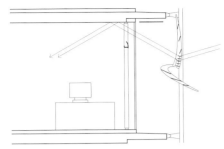

50 a Daylight control on south side
in sunshine

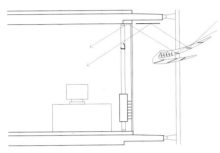

b Daylight control on south side
under an overcast sky

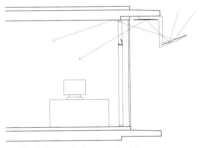

c Daylight control on north side
under an overcast sky

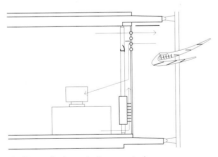

d Controlled, centrally operated
natural ventilation

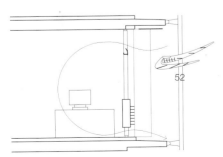

e free ventilation
with open ventilation sashes

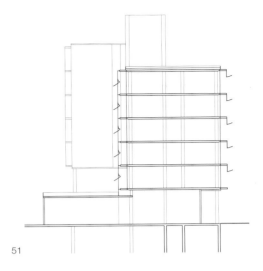

51

48 Site plan   scale 1:10 000
49 View of north facade
50 Daylight control and ventilation
51 Cross-section   scale 1:500
52 Interior view of facade

Next page: View of south facade

52

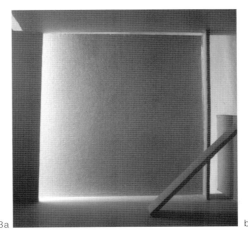

53a                                          b

## Design Tools

Simulations of the light conditions conducted during the design stage can give reliable insights into the delivery of daylight and the light ambience of a space. They are used to optimise proposals.

*Models*

A good method of simulation is the architectural model. Since light has extremely short wavelengths (compared to other measurements in our environment), scale is of no consequence (in contrast to other physical processes such as heat propagation or room acoustics). It does not matter if the model is at a scale of 1:1, 1:20 or 1:50 – the amount and distribution of light, and the light ambience remain the same, providing the outdoor conditions are the same. Essentially, the geometric proportions, colouring and surface properties of the model must be accurate.
With the help of a miniature camera placed inside the 1:20 scale model (sometimes even 1:50 is sufficient) realistic photographs can be taken.
However, the problem is where to find the right sky. Ideally, an artificial sky should be used which can simulate clear skies, as well as overcast conditions of different days and all seasons. The availability of such equipment is limited in Germany.
The question of when the sun will shine where can be answered with a simple sun simulator. An exact parallel beam is set at the correct angle to the model, depending on time of day and season. Internal and external shading may then be photographed.
If one places the model outside, under an overcast sky, the camera will record the correct illumination within the space. This is also true on sunny days, although running this type of simulation for a whole year would be rather time-consuming.
A model workshop may also be used. A few ceiling washers represent the (overcast or clear) sky and the sun is represented by a spotlight bundling light effectively (e.g. halogen lamp). Of course this simple method, which can be employed by anyone, does not produce correct information on the amount of light in the interior of the model. Nonetheless, information on the quality of daylight on overcast days and in sunshine (play of light and shadow) is telling, and difficult to convey in ever so complex computer programmes.

*Computer simulation*

Another method of obtaining preliminary simulations involves the use of computer programmes.
Modern CAD programmes give the option of calculating shadows cast by the sun. All other simulation of the light situation under different sky conditions is simplified because of the otherwise lengthy computing times. The resultant false colour representation will give an impression of the illumination, but does not provide accurate information on the amount of light and its distribution (the image is brightened – dark areas, for example, are not recognised or shown). In terms of conveying the light ambience these images do not reach the same standard as simple model photography.
Of course there are light simulation programmes that compute near accurate representations of the atmospheric quality of light. The rule is: the more accurate and high-quality the image, the longer the computing time and the operator's input. The all-rounder in this field is RADIANCE, which has several user interfaces (also see p. 57ff). The complexity of the programme makes it advisable to commission special consultants or institutes for this task.
Simpler programmes that are easy to operate are much better suited to architects. These cannot do everything, but are extremely useful at the design development stage. They are best employed in the comparison of different design options to optimise a proposal. A selection of these programmes (for example, PRIMERO_Licht) is listed in the Appendix (see pp. 104, 105). This list, while not claiming completeness, is a representation of the current situation, and future developments should be watched closely.

left: View of south facade, administration building in Wiesbaden
53  a, b  Artists' studio, student project (see p. 27). The model photographs show the view from the main window (NE) to the interior of the building. Narrow slits give the space a special light ambiance.
The photographs simulate the situation on a sunny day in spring/autumn.
(a: morning, b: noon).

# Daylight Control

Ulrike Brandi

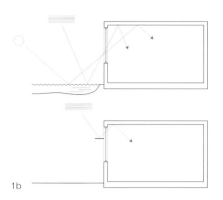

1b

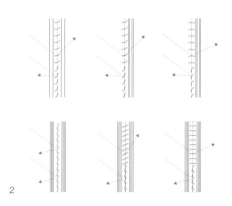

2

During the past two decades daylight planning has been established in the performance profile of lighting designers. Clients and architects are starting to understand the influence of daylight, in all its facets. Today, teams of specialists design building skins: architects, HVAC engineers and energy consultants, facade and lighting designers. We, the lighting designers, simulate the proposed building geometry, either with models and an artificial sky, or by using simulation software. Both of these tools have advantages and disadvantages, but can be used to complement one another. During the past 20 years, daylight has also become an important consideration for engineers. The drive to save energy has set off a search for ways to maximise the effective use of daylight while at the same time reducing the associated – in most cases unfavourable – thermal radiation. The recent association of the two disciplines of daylight planning and indoor climate technology has yet to be put into architectural practice – an interesting prospect. In addition to the ecological and economic advantages of a good supply of daylight in a building, planned use of natural light enhances design and has a positive effect on the physical and psychological well-being of its users. The qualities of natural light are irreplaceable. Hence, examining the existing daylight conditions should be the starting point of every artificial lighting scheme. The first clues will be derived from the building's orientation, its location and surroundings, and the shading to which it will be subject. The requirements of a building will differ according to its geographic location: in northern latitudes, where there is less available sunlight and warmth, the extensive utilisation of light is essential. The closer we are to the equator, the more daylight there is and the more closed-off the architecture will be.

*Principles of daylight systems*
Apart from the significant effect daylight has on the landscape and on urban spaces, it also determines the authentic site of a building. For this reason, it is of utmost importance to engage architects and clients in a detailed discussion on the intended role of daylight. Well-planned, imaginative use of daylight will strengthen the character of a building and create a unique atmosphere that will change through the course of a day and through the seasons while serving a wide range of functions. Initially it is helpful to establish the most extreme solar radiation conditions, at noon throughout the year, and at dawn and dusk. In addition, different weather conditions have to be taken into account: bright sunlight, overcast sky, fog, twilight, brilliant autumn weather, thunderstorms, rain or snow. In some instances the sun needs to be filtered out, in others the natural light needs supplementing with artificial light. Changing light conditions have a positive influence on the well-being of people (see p. 8f). For many years, attempts have been made to set a standard for ergonomically "correct" lighting. This has led to a monotonous uniformity of illuminance levels and

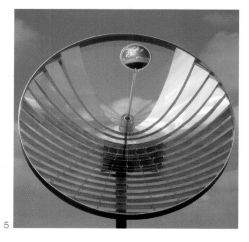

5

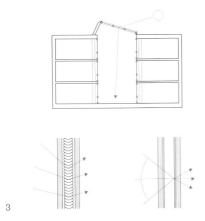

3

4

1     Simple daylight control
2     Light deflecting louvres and Venetian blinds
3     Lighting-control glass for roofs or facades
4, 5   Heliostat for light deflection
6     Model simulation of New Mercedes Benz
      Museum, Stuttgart (see p. 57ff)
      Architects: UN Studio van Berkel & Bos,
      Amsterdam
      Daylight Design: Transsolar Energietechnik and
      ULRIKE BRANDI LICHT

a reduction in contrasts and reflectance, especially in offices. Today, we increasingly design for dynamic lighting situations, even in office spaces, integrating as much daylight as possible. Studies of people's waking and sleep rhythms, and health problems such as SAD (Seasonal Affective Disorder) common in northern latitudes, SBS (Sick Building Syndrome) and ADD (Attention Deficit Disorder) found that the supply of sufficient daylight is vital. Daylight is far superior in quality and intensity to artificial light; on sunny days we will find 10 000 to 100 000 lux outdoors. A further characteristic affecting people is the varying spectral composition of light. Traditional methods of controlling and deflecting daylight are often simple but compare well with many of the technically complex systems created during the last twenty years. A deep, white painted window soffit deflects daylight into the room. Even the glazing bars of old windows will deflect light onto the ceiling of an interior space – and these windows, despite their comparatively small glazed area, are, in terms of daylight, only slightly less effective than larger windows. A pool of water adjacent to a building will reflect daylight into the interior (Figure 1a).

Light shelves reflect daylight onto the ceilings of interior spaces and also protect areas close to the windows from exposure to direct sunlight (Figure 1 b).

### Solar glazing
The 1970s saw the introduction of solar glazing. This type of glass is coated to filter out thermal radiation and the infrared spectral range of sunlight. However, the glass often has a strong dimming effect, making interior spaces appear gloomy, especially when the weather is bad. It has a mirror-like appearance on the outside and can cause glare in neighbouring buildings. Also available is glass with a reduced dimming effect and an appearance closer to clear glass, but this is less effective. It is often used in skylights and glazed roofs of halls.
Stove-enamelled glass offers many variations and can be applied as a partial or graduated coating. A fine grid on a glazed roof is hardly visible from below and does not appreciably influence the transparency of the glass.

### Louvres and Venetian blinds
Horizontal louvres and Venetian blinds enable precise control of light. Sunlight

can be entirely filtered out or deflected onto the ceiling in order to direct it far into an interior space (Figure 2). Various materials for coating the slats are available and can enhance this effect. External blinds are susceptible to wind damage but internal blinds are less effective in terms of thermal protection. Venetian blinds can also be fixed in the cavity of double-glazing where they do not collect dirt as easily. Louvres on the facade – made of anodised aluminium or glass – can take on larger dimensions and a variety of cross-sections. The arched, reflecting surface fans out the light.

### Lighting-control glass
There are several systems that use the space between the panes of double-glazing to accommodate optimised optical objects and profiles. Light-control glass is filled with acrylic sections that deflect light onto the ceiling of an interior space by means of total reflection within the acrylic material. An additional prismatic contouring of the inner pane of glass helps to distribute lower altitude light in a room (Figure 3).

### Prismatic sheets in double glazing
Prismatic sheets also rely on total reflection in acrylic glass: While direct sunlight is reflected back to the outside or against the ceiling of an interior space, diffuse light from the sky passes through the material. Prismatic sheets are used in windows and skylights. They can be combined in up to three layers of differently shaped prisms and are occasionally used with partially mirror-evaporated prism sides to guarantee protection against solar radiation, glare and deflection for various positions of the sun. However, they are expensive and absorb much light, hence, lighting designers have been searching for alternative methods. Prism slats are of simpler construction and may

6

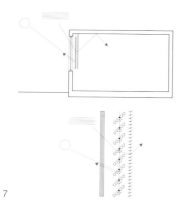

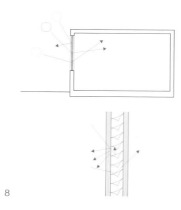

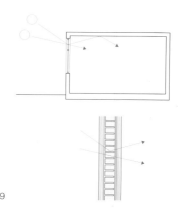

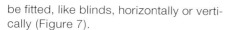

7

8

9

be fitted, like blinds, horizontally or vertically (Figure 7).

*Mirror sections in double glazing*
Mirror profiles are inserted into the double glazing cavity. The differently shaped parabolic mirrors are arranged to admit the low-altitude winter sunlight while deflecting the summer sun entering at a steeper angle (Figure 8). The profiles are rigid and custom-formed to respond to the respective cardinal points and installation methods. They are installed on facades and roofs.

*Laser-Cut Panels (LCP)*
LCP are used as fixed systems within the double glazing cavity of clerestory windows or as pivoting elements in front of facades. Small, laser-cut incisions on the surface of acrylic glass deflect sunlight (Figure 9). All LCP systems interfere, to some degree, with the view out and are only used in roofs or skylights.

*Holographic-Optical Elements (HOE)*
The specifically designed optics of HOE are used as sun protection. Holographic film is embedded between layers of laminated glass to deflect light. In the process of refraction, light is split into its spectral colours, which is counteracted by the slight diffusing property of the glass. Because HOE are only effective for a limited range of angles, different types of HOE may be used side by side or above one another to deflect sunlight away from the upper part of the glazed areas of facades or skylights.

*Heliostats*
Heliostats are mirrors that "follow" the sun to deflect its rays in a certain direction. Sunlight can be redirected, e.g. from the roof of a building via a courtyard into its lower storeys (Figures 4, 5). Ordinary heliostats need to move in two directions

as the sun moves from east to west while changing its altitude. The heliostat mechanism requires substantial maintenance and the effect depends on the size of the light-catching mirror. The illustration shows a heliostat consisting of an asymmetrical parabolic mirror that is subdivided into segments and placed between sheets of glass. Its mechanism is much simpler than that of ordinary heliostats, as it merely revolves around its own axis in the course of one day. The refraction of direct sunlight into an interior space can have astonishingly brilliant results, but is only effective on sunny days. Many sys-

tems have objectionable side effects, such as splitting white sunlight into its spectral colours, or make patterns such as striped prisms or squares created by the dovetailing of single plates. These details may not suit all styles of architecture.

The daylight systems introduced here require further development. Often a simple layout is all that is required to accomplish successful daylight control for an interior space. Early involvement of the lighting designer in the project is an essential part of sound daylight planning.

10

11

12

*Daylight simulation using models*
Models can be used to gain detailed insight into daylight conditions. A light source with parallel rays is used to simulate the sun. Parabolic mirrors able to produce this type of ray pattern are generally 0.6 to 1.0 m in diameter. For the model to be completely "sunlit" it needs to be smaller in size than the mirror. The artificial sun can then be adjusted to simulate all possible locations and times, even entire days can be run through in quick motion. For the design of the Mercedes Benz Museum in Stuttgart (Figure 6, also see p. 57ff) model simulations at a scale of 1:24 were supplemented by computer calculations. The geometrically complex building offers astonishing vistas and some surprising light incidences from certain angles. In transitions between the darker museum spaces and those receiving daylight we investigated the luminous density of the facades in order to determine whether glare will occur, in both sunny and overcast conditions. Furthermore, it was important to determine how far sunlight would reach into the exhibition space and to what degree the central atrium would provide daylight within the interior spaces. In winter, the low sun penetrates nearly the entire space, while on summer days only the facade receives direct sunlight. Computer renderings can produce the exact daylight factor, luminance factor and illuminance. A model, however, creates an impression of a space and the anticipated atmosphere within, even if the materials and reflectance values will change in the course of the design process.

*Daylight and artificial light for the entrance hall at the University of Bremen*
In the new entrance hall at the University of Bremen we used daylight control technology for redirecting daylight and artificial light. The University of Bremen com-

prises numerous exposed aggregate concrete buildings dating from the 1970s which have an appearance that is incongruent with modern university life. To provide a central entrance space the architects Alsop + Störmer designed a glazed hall occupying the area between existing buildings and linking these via a 'boulevard' (Figure 10). An orange grid was imprinted on the roof glazing; a few panes were left clear and transparent. These transparent panes contain holographic-optical elements (HOE) that deflect light from exterior spotlights into the hall. The hall is free of luminaires. Five spotlights on the glass roof provide the basic illumination at night. Their maintenance is not a problem despite the great height, since they are mounted on the roof (Figures 11,12). HOE not only deflect the beams of light, but also separate the light into its spectral colours and project these onto the floor of the hall. The manufacture of HOE involves exposing holographic film to an interference pattern of laser beams. When the film is developed, the interference pattern is fixed as a continuous layout of dissimilar refractive indices. Light arising from any weather conditions can be adjusted and redirected. HOE, like film layers in ordinary laminated security glass, are embedded between the panes. Laminated security glass fitted with an HOE layer combines the known properties and advantages of ordinary laminated security glass with the new light-control technology. Additional object lighting is used to emphasise certain areas and also to supplement the general lighting. The striking V-shaped pillars receive narrow, focussed beams of light, making the supporting structure of the building visible from the outside against a low level basic illumination. The walls of the stairwell present an animated interplay of light and dark surfaces. The rear wall is faced with black slate – in front of it

7   Prismatic sheets behind glazing
8   Mirror sections in panes of double glazing
9   Laser-cut panels
10–12   Entrance hall at the University of Bremen;
        Architects: Alsop + Störmer, Hamburg
        Lighting Design: ULRIKE BRANDI LICHT

14　　15

a wall, evenly lit from above, is superimposed on the dark surface. Additionally, recessed wall luminaires provide indirect light to the peripheral areas of the generously dimensioned stairs. Light diodes are randomly scattered across the floor to mark the main circulation routes.

*Daylight planning at the LVA (State Insurance), Administrative Headquarters Hamburg:*
The building is glazed on all sides; a generously proportioned courtyard is diagonally dissected by a pathway. The new building for the LVA had to meet functional needs as well as provide a pleasant environment (Figure 13). Uninterrupted sight lines and circulation routes create a communication space, a design principle adopted by the daylight concept. The aim was to maximise comfort in the interior spaces and to utilise daylight, the natural resource, to its optimum effect. The brief required the space to be provided with a

bright, uniform and colour-neutral illumination using natural light for a maximum number of daytime hours. The question of sufficient daylight supply was not the only relevant issue since all offices include computer workstations. All spaces are completely glazed in, on the outside as well as the inside, making it necessary to examine direct sunlight and luminous densities from the sky in the areas near windows. In addition, some of the windows to the courtyard have a mirror-like appearance when viewed from the offices opposite so that even spaces facing north receive direct sunlight. We analysed the daylight conditions of a standard office located in the outer, western zone of the building (Figure 14). In these rooms unwanted glare was caused by direct sunlight, the contrast between bright and dark surfaces, or by indirect light (reflection). German standard (DIN 5034 Part 1) and the EU directive for computer workstations identify the following objectives:

13

16

- good glare protection, i.e. not exceeding 400 cd/m²
- clear lines of vision to provide a connection to the outdoors, crucial for mental well-being
- efficient use of the resource daylight using daylight control
- high degree of daylight autonomy, i.e. long periods of use when artificial light is not required.

In consultation with the architects and other facade specialists, we opted for internal Venetian blinds with concave, 80 mm duplex slats, perforated on one half with 0.7 mm diameter holes at a perforation rate of approximately 6%. The slats are colour coated (RAL 7030) on the rear face and have a lustre of 10–20% (Figure 17). We presumed the point of observation to be a seated user at a distance of 2.50 m (and height of 1.15 m) from the window. To calculate the daylight factor we used the rotation symmetrical CIE sky model, as defined by DIN 5034 Part 2, as a light source. This is the only sky model that reproduces lighting conditions in interior spaces. The investigation of possible glare is also important. The simulation shows that the lowest luminance occurs in the primary glare zone

when the slats are shut (horizontal line of vision to window). The maximum allowable value of 400 cd/m², set by the EU directive, is not exceeded. Comparison of the two situations clearly shows the difference in luminance with the anti-glare screen in an open or closed position (Figures 15, 16). To avoid unwanted reflection on the computer screens, the user would have to completely close the slats as soon as the sun shone on the facade. This would reduce the illuminance to a level below 300 lx in almost all daylight conditions and, to comply with standard DIN EN 12464, artificial lights would have to be switched on. To avoid this, the upper quarter sections of the windows are used for daylight control. The slats in an open position deflect daylight onto the ceiling, from where it is reflected deep into the space. The illuminance is raised to approximately 300 lx and is distributed more uniformly than before. Users of the LVA offices can regulate the daylight to suit their preferences. The offices achieve daylight autonomy for approximately 85% of the main working hours from 9:00 am to 5:00 pm, thereby keeping the energy consumption and the removal of the resultant heat at a low level.

13 Administrative offices LVA, Hamburg, 2002
   Architects: Schweger und Partner, Hamburg
   Lighting Design: ULRIKE BRANDI LICHT
14 Typical office on west elevation
15 Luminance when anti-glare screen open
16 Luminance when anti-glare screen closed
17 Perforated and coated duplex slats

Ulrike Brandi is managing director of ULRIKE BRANDI LICHT, founded in Hamburg in 1986, consultants and designers for artificial lighting and daylight design.
Numerous lectures and publications, including "Light Book – The Practice of Lighting Design".

17

## Light for the Public Utility Company in Schönebeck

Ulrike Brandi

1

The Public Utility Company in Schönebeck wanted a new energy-efficient building. Clever design with daylight can have an impact here, just as it can improve the quality of light in workplaces. Severe traffic pollution at the site, building regulations, and the company's ecological objectives led to the design of a compact inward-facing building. Two solid building sections flank a glazed hall that forms the centre in terms of function, energy and daylight. Facing the interior space are offices, counter workplaces and circulation areas (waiting zone and exhibition space on the ground floor, cafeteria on the first floor and an auditorium on the second floor), while the secondary functions, such as sanitary facilities, copy and storage rooms, are located, as a "buffer", in the outer zones of the solid building sections.

### Daylight

We studied the light radiation penetrating the glazed atrium (Figures 2–7) to ascertain whether the workplaces would obtain sufficient amounts of daylight, whether the sunlight would lead to unacceptable levels of glare and heat gain, and as the case may be to establish measures to improve the situation.

We found that the east-west orientation of the hall and the southerly incline of the glazed roof generally suited the utilisation concept of the building. The sunlight penetrating the glazed roof at a steep angle permits the desired solar gain and offers a lively abundance of light in the atrium. At the same time, discomfort at the workplaces is negligible as sunlight mainly falls onto circulation spaces. The use of colour-neutral solar glazing in combination with printed panes in the roof (white dot screen with 30 % shading), in conjunction with the thermal storage properties of the solid building sections and a ventilation concept, are sufficient to ensure a pleasant indoor climate.

Even in the problematic glazed entrance area to the west (low altitude of the sun in the afternoon) it could be demonstrated that apart form solar glazing no additional measures, such as external louvres, would have to be taken. The floor plan helped: the lift core next to the entrance and the projecting oriel shield the office areas beyond from glare. The orientation of the EDP workplaces towards the hall also prevents glare, as the light comes from the side, not from the front or back of the screens.

We also examined the possibility of directing more daylight into the building. The west facade in particular, where office workplaces are located, would be suitable for deflecting daylight using holographic optical elements or light-deflecting louvres in the interspace of double glazing. The cost-benefit analysis results were not convincing. Due to its favourable geometry, the central atrium of the Public Utility Company in Schönebeck receives high levels of daylight during working hours, only rarely requiring artificial lights to be switched on.

The concept of a glass hall flooded with light, forming the green heart of the building, could be implemented with a relatively low technical input; and because the findings of the daylight analysis were incorporated at the design stage.

Client: Stadtwerke Schönebeck
Architects: Günther Haß and
Stefan Rimpf, Eckernförde
Artificial lighting and daylight design:
ULRIKE BRANDI LICHT

1   Public Utility Company in Schönebeck, west facade
2–4 The sections illustrate the direct incident solar radiation through the south facing glass roof throughout the seasons and days. It shows that adverse optical effects are negligible in the workplaces because sunlight mainly hits the circulation areas.
5–7 The solar radiation on the east and west facade can be checked in plan. Sunlight hits the EDP workplaces oriented towards the glazed hall laterally, that is, neither from the front nor from behind, causing only marginal glare. Parts of the building (lift core and projection) shade the workplaces to a great extent from the critical, low altitude sun.

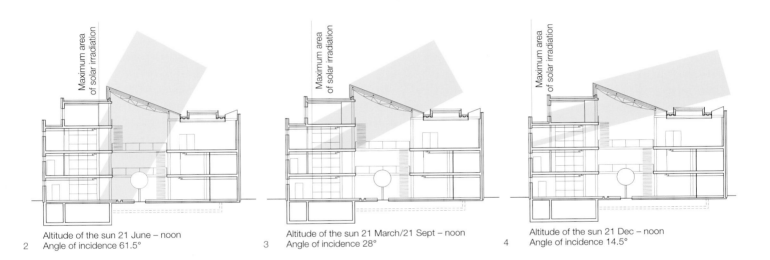

Altitude of the sun 21 June – noon
2   Angle of incidence 61.5°

Altitude of the sun 21 March/21 Sept – noon
3   Angle of incidence 28°

Altitude of the sun 21 Dec – noon
4   Angle of incidence 14.5°

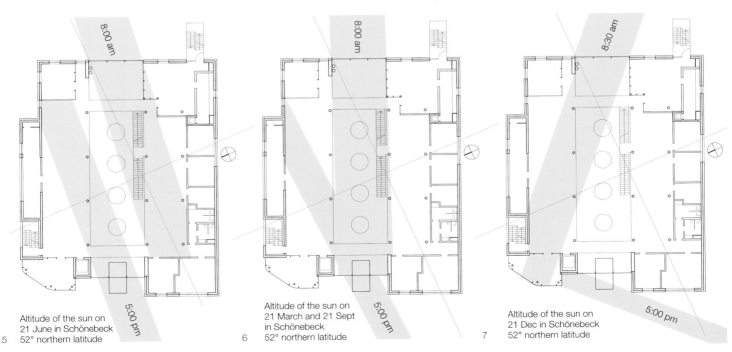

Altitude of the sun on
21 June in Schönebeck
5   52° northern latitude

Altitude of the sun on
21 March and 21 Sept
in Schönebeck
6   52° northern latitude

Altitude of the sun on
21 Dec in Schönebeck
7   52° northern latitude

8a

b

**Artificial light**

*The hall*
The impression created by illumination of the generously proportioned hall is accomplished by lighting the two flanking office tracts. Bright ceilings visually extend the atrium and create a friendly atmosphere. Scaled-down inconspicuous pendant luminaires achieve, with a combination of direct and indirect light, bright ceilings and differentiated pleasant light for working in. The luminaires, positioned perpendicular to the axis of the hall, are slender in appearance and do not obstruct the view into the space beyond.

The light in the galleries' circulation areas is different from that of the offices: surface-mounted downlights with softly deflecting diffuse glass are visible light sources lined up beneath the galleries. The pendant luminaires that provide the general lighting in the hall do not disrupt the impression of the space. They are sober and technical in character.

The walls flanking the entrance area to the west are lit from below by recessed floor luminaires and by surface-mounted spotlights from the top, giving emphasis to the entry zone.
In the evening ambience, small spotlights beneath the glazed roof highlight its construction, thereby marking the limits of the space. Recessed floor lights illuminate the trees to create a special atmosphere for nighttime events.
Light points on the pool amplify the movement of the water, adding a playful and lively aspect that even extends to the exterior.

*Office areas*
The light of the office spaces, with pendant luminaires, has been described above. It is supplemented by surface-mounted downlights which are visible only as round light apertures. These shed a wash of light from above across the rear walls of the offices and limit the space as seen from the hall.
Due to the backlighting, the fully glazed north-west facade maintains a strong presence in the streetscape.

*The auditorium*
Two lighting systems integrated into the ceiling, create both sober light for meetings and lectures and festive light for nighttime events. The latter is emitted from dimmable recessed luminaires; the former is reflected by large white reflec-

tors in the luminaires. Compact fluorescent lamps intensify the effect. An inconspicuously placed line of light along the skylight and the band of windows the length of the outside wall emphasise this area in the evening.

*Cafeteria*
Downlights with opal covers alternate with pendant luminaires to create atmospheric light in the cafeteria. Where the gallery meets the cafeteria, the gallery lighting is deliberately continued to maintain its clarity when seen from the hall.
The sanitary facilities receive light from diffuse deflecting surface-mounted luminaires in combination with two vertical luminaires mounted on either side of the mirror. Auxiliary rooms are lit by fluorescent luminaires with opal covers.

*External stairs*
Recessed wall luminaires brighten the underside of the steps above and highlight the verticality as viewed from the outside.

Fluorescent lamps and high pressure discharge lamps were predominantly used as were light diodes, which are energy-efficient and low maintenance. In some areas additional luminaires with tungsten halogen lamps were fitted for extra brilliant light.
The luminaires are controlled and adjusted via an EIB system.

8  a, b  Public Utility Company Schönebeck, Atrium
One of the determining factors of the light ambience in the hall was the choice of solar glazing. Only colour-neutral glass prevents distortion of natural colours and also artificial light colours as well as other unwanted effects (often a greenish tinge).
Panes in the roof glazing are printed with a fine white dot screen shading 30 % of the area. They are hardly visible from below and do not obscure the transparency of the glass.

## Light and Shadow –
## Design of a Church

Christina Augustesen

Attuning a design to daylight requires incorporating the animated play of shadows. Shadows as strong design elements that have yet to receive enough attention. Depending on the light incidence shadows can move, intensify, or produce different colour effects in the eye of the beholder. While artificial light is generally static and almost like a snapshot, a continually changing light ambience is alive.

*What is shadow?*
Shadow is, according to the metaphor, "a hole in the light, something absent". The light seems to be absent, but the shadow proves the existence of light by negating it.
Near shadows, light has only one direction. Shadows describe the appearance of the objects that have cast them. This leads to active moments of perception, although the shadow remains passive. The object produces the shadow, and as the object moves, the shadow changes, not vice versa. Shadows are always two-dimensional; they fall onto surfaces which may well form part of a spatial arrangement. If space on a horizontal plane is not sufficient, the shadow will transfer to an inclined or vertical plane behind. Shadow does not have a predetermined direction or predefined shape, it is pliant.

If the shadow falls onto differently positioned surfaces, horizontal or vertical for example, a separate spatial impression is perceived in each situation. Light and darkness produce diverse spatial effects. Spaces that are alive with moving shadows will be perceived in a more differentiated manner than spaces with fixed lighting.

Shadows occur fleetingly and can quickly change. The shadow follows the occurrence of light and intensifies in parallel to its expressiveness. A direct ray of sun-

light will draw a sharply outlined silhouette; diffuse light of the overcast sky hardly produces shadows at all. When daylight fades so do the shadows and the illuminated room will retain its contours.

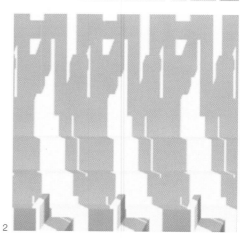

The shadows in a room are the result of sunlight passing through the window with its glazing bars, across the furniture, colours and surfaces and into the room. Shadows vary according to the position of sunlight, following in sequence. The shadows of visitors are superimposed; their shadows overlap with the shadows of the objects in the room, blending into one image.
Some shadows can be calculated in advance. However, other shadows can quickly alter their shape, while always remaining a mystery to the eye; they succeed in fascinating us.

The mystery of shadows and the quality of daylight were the source of inspiration for the design of the church in Trekroner, Denmark.

1–4 Light studies using 3D computer models are an important instrument in the design process to examine different alternatives.
5 Sectional elevation facing altar
6 Sectional elevation facing organ
7 Floor plan
8 Longitudinal section

## Concept

The space of the church is of a simple composition. The liveliness is produced by the incidence of light and the resultant shadows which change continuously. Thus the design follows the traditions of religious architecture.

Light, as a possible metaphor, makes the church accessible to the believer as a worldly manifestation of divinity; it describes the cycle of life in a daily recurring rhythm of light incidence in its endless variations. The space was conceived as a "protective cover" to provide the visitor with a safe environment for prayer and concentration. The universe is present in the shadows.

Rhythm and repetition are important elements for Christians in finding a deeper relationship with themselves and the divinity. In this sense, the design is traditional: The rhythm of the structure creates light and shadow in a cycle of daily renewable nuances.

## Light and spatial structure

The church is sited according to Christian tradition along the points of the compass: the longitudinal facades are north-south orientated, the vestibule to the west and the chancel to the east.

The exterior of the church is shaped like a glass cube held by the closed ends at the vestibule (14 m in height) and the chancel (19 m in height).

In the interior, the supporting timber construction arches like a perforated shell across the church space, its effect constantly changing with the shadows.

Heavy concrete walls, with 4 to 5 metre-high steps that could be described as side aisles, enclose the lower third of the space. The steps can be used for additional seating and form the southern part of the gallery which can be reached from the vestibule. The opaque sections of the interior walls are projection surfaces for

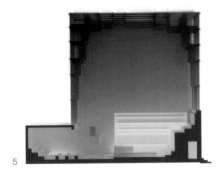

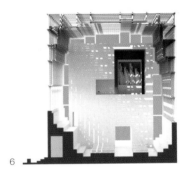

5

6

a Vestibule
b Baptistery
c Chapel
d Altar
e Sacristy

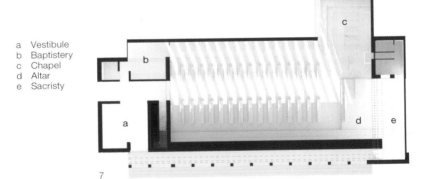

7

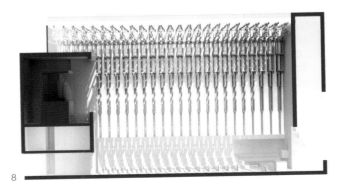

8

# Light for the New Mercedes Benz Museum in Stuttgart

ULRIKE BRANDI LICHT

The footprint of the New Mercedes Benz Museum is a simple geometric shape. An equilateral triangle with rounded corners comprises three circles, a small central atrium marks the centre. In section this is developed into a dynamic sequence of ramps and levels with glazed areas in which the collection is housed, and closed-off "mythos" spaces are reserved for special exhibitions (Figures 4, 5).

The collection area has a ceiling height of approximately 4.5 metres and displays vehicles in a daylight atmosphere similar to that outside, where one would expect to find them. The facade lets filtered daylight into the building, the Stuttgart landscape recedes into a backdrop for the exhibits. The ceiling is smooth and bright, reminiscent of the sky. Integrated lighting elements give off direct light, like rays of sunlight penetrating the clouds (clouds luminaire, see p. 74ff).

The "mythos" spaces, in contrast, are designed to receive little daylight and so use artificial lighting to stage the "myths" in a theatre-like setting.

The aim of this daylight design is to reinforce the architect's and exhibition designer's concept. The quality of the light distribution and quantity of light in the museum is assessed with the help of computer-generated daylight simulations and models. Information on the building's exposure to the sun, required by all exhibition designers, artificial-lighting consultants, HVAC engineers and also landscape architects, was used to produce a shading study.

## Principles of daylight design

The objective of daylight design is to enhance user comfort and to reduce power consumption for lighting and cooling. In this context, the term user-comfort does not stand for luxury but for the "quality necessary for our well-being".

Specifically, this means providing uniform, colour-neutral daylight in interior spaces for a maximum number of hours per day, protection from glare and overheating from solar radiation, and spacious rooms with a pronounced relationship to the outdoors.

In the design of buildings with a specialised function, like the proposed New Mercedes Benz Museum, some of these principles may fall behind other objectives, such as the architectural design or the exhibition concept.

The illuminance, uniformity of light distribution and related light technical comfort values are defined as minimum values in standards and directives (DIN 5034, DIN 5035 or DIN EN 12464). These are supplemented by the lighting designer's recommendation for good daylight delivery in interior spaces. Nonetheless, each individual will have a different perception of the light situation and with it the degree of contentment will vary.

One of the often underestimated advantages of daylight is its great capacity. The luminous efficacy of the available output is greater than that of any artificial light source; daylight is also the "coolest" light for the illumination of interior spaces as it produces – if utilised correctly – the lowest thermal loads.

The appropriate protection from overheating will result in a lower cooling load and, hence, a smaller system requiring shorter operating times for ventilation and cooling. The shading system employed will decrease daylight delivery to the interior. It must be ensured that sufficient daylight penetrates the room when the system is closed, to avoid the use of additional artificial lighting.

The energy balance can also be improved with the use of selective solar glazing that admits much light into the room but little

New Mercedes Benz Museum,
Stuttgart, 2006
General contractor: DaimlerChrysler
Immobilien, Berlin
Architect: UN Studio van Berkel & Bos, Amsterdam
Exhibition design: HG Merz, Stuttgart
Daylight design: Transsolar Energietechnik,
Stuttgart and ULRIKE BARNDI LICHT, Hamburg

energy. The selectivity index S indicates the rating of solar glazing in terms of a high light transmittance (t) in proportion to a desired low total energy transmittance (g). A high selectivity index is desirable. For glazing products a value approaching S = 2 represents the physical limits (see p. 30).

Another essential factor influencing well-being is the colour of light and the colour changes during the course of the day. Evolution compels us to perceive natural daylight as the most pleasant kind of light; it can only be partly substituted by

artificial light. Hence, it is important that glazing does not cause significant colour changes in interior spaces. The colour rendering properties of glazing are assessed using the colour rendition index Ra according to the standard DIN 6169 or DIN EN 410. The Ra scale extends up to 100. The optimum for glazing is a Ra value of 99.

### Requirements for the illumination of interior spaces

*Luminance, illuminance and daylight factor*
Luminance is the measure of brightness perceived by the eye from a luminous or

lit surface (see p. 17). It is dependent on the direction of view and is measured in candela per unit area ($cd/m^2$).

Illuminance, in contrast, defines the total luminous flux falling onto a certain area – irrespective of what the eye perceives (see p. 18). It is measured in lux (lx).

Daylight factor D is a design value and measurement also used in assessing the quality of daylight in interior spaces. The standard DIN 5034 "Daylight in Interiors" states: $D = E_p/E_a$. The daylight factor is the ratio of illuminance $E_p$ at a certain

1

2

point in an interior space to the illuminance Ea outdoors at that time without being affected by obstructions. In contrast to artificial lighting, daylight is not constant but depends on factors such as cloud cover, altitude of the sun, atmospheric haze and shading devices on the building.

Since only an overcast sky has a typical rotation-symmetrical distribution of luminance, this is the sole light condition that can be simulated for interior spaces. A clear sky and direct sunlight are necessary for the assessment of the momentary illuminance, especially when analysing the occurrence of glare. In this context the daylight factor is not an accurate representation. The overcast sky (in Germany approximately 50 % of the time) is the more critical condition in light-technical terms because the darker sky is the basis for the design of daylight schemes (see p. 22ff).

*Recommended values for daylight delivery*
The standard DIN 5034-1 sets a minimum daylight factor, for office space only, which should be adhered to. The only other guides are found in the illuminance levels required in interior spaces using artificial lighting, according to standard DIN 5035 (DIN EN 12464).

Recommendations for the nominal illuminance of the ambient illumination are 300 or 500 lx (see p. 18). Hence, a daylight factor of 3 or 5 % should initially be aimed for, so that daylight and artificial lighting are balanced under overcast sky conditions (diffuse sky of 10 000 lx).

*Uniformity of light distribution*
Another criterion for good daylight conditions is the uniformity G of the daylight factor.
In the standard DIN 5034-6 it is defined as the ratio of minimal to average daylight factor, therefore uniformity $G = D_{min}/D_{avg}$.

The minimum value is the lowest daylight factor in an area (horizontal usable floor space 0.85 m above floor level). For rooms with lateral windows a ratio of 1:4 is good; at $G < 1:10$, the uniformity is insufficient. The uniformity for rooms with skylights should not fall below 1:2.

1  Exhibition space „collection", model at scale
   1:24 for daylight simulation
2  Exhibition space „collection", simulation of
   sunlight on a model

3

3  Exhibition space "collection",
   south side, simulation of the altitudes of the sun
   on a model, scale 1:24
4  Floor plan of typical storey
5  Elevation, extent of daylight study

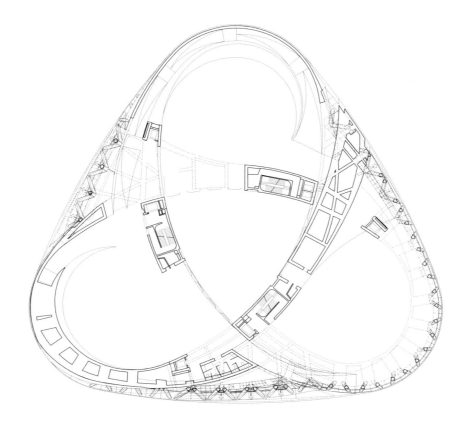

4

5

43.14 m

36.00 m

21.96 m

5.58 m

47.16 m

26.64 m

11.34 m

## Principles of daylight simulation

Special computer programmes can calculate the light quantity and light distribution, and – with the required computing input – also simulate the quality of the light atmosphere (see p. 41). The light calculation programme RELUX is widely used.

*Simulation programme RADIANCE*
RADIANCE is a programme that was developed at the Lawrence Berkeley National Laboratory (USA) for the calculation of light propagation and light distribution in complex geometries. Computation of daylight as well as artificial lighting is possible. The results may be in the form of individual light-technical values, such as illuminance at a specific point of reference, or luminance in the observer's field of vision. Photo-realistic visualisations of interior spaces are also possible, providing the full light-technical information in each pixel.

RADIANCE calculations were thoroughly tested and confirmed by comparative measuring around the world. The programme is currently one of the high-performance tools for lighting simulations, and was employed in the design of the New Mercedes Benz Museum. Because the programme is highly complex and time-consuming, it is seldom used by planning professionals. The computing procedure is briefly described in the following.

*Geometry of a space*
The geometry of a space is composed of a few simple basic volumes (polygons, spheres, cubes, etc.) of any number and at every scale. Any shape can be produced at the required degree of detail. The programme is able to convert 3D-DXF files from CAD applications.

*Light sources*
Sky models are employed to represent the light source in daylight calculations, the standard being the CIE sky according to DIN 5034-2.

*Method of calculation*
The programme works on a "backward ray tracing" algorithm. The method traces rays from the viewpoint into a mathematical 3D model of the scene, reflected on surfaces, transmitted or absorbed and traced back to the light sources. In contrast to forward ray tracing, not all rays emitted by a source must be traced but only those that actually reach the viewpoint.

This method computes luminance on the basis of predefined illuminances and daylight factors.

## Daylight simulation for the New Mercedes Benz Museum

*Requirements*
The exact position of the proposed building is required to set up the sky model employed in the daylight simulation. The New Mercedes Benz Museum, Stuttgart, lies at 9°14' eastern longitude and 48°48' northern latitude.

The reflectance of all opaque surfaces is 50%, the light transmittance of glazing also 50%.

6 Interior view of model, scale 1:24, view of the critical daylight transition zones between "mythos" and "collection" spaces.

6

7

8

9

7–9   Shading study on a model, scale 1:24,
       for December, March, June – at noon.
       The study shows how daylight enters the
       interior space and its influence on exhibits.
10–12  Daylight study "mythos" section:
       The model shows, for each individual spatial
       situation (different levels, different orienta-
       tion), all the areas which are critical in terms
       of daylight.
13     Shading study model for a sun protection
       system on the building's facade (not imple-
       mented).

10          11          12

*First studies of the daylight characteristics of the museum*

The daylight factor is established in horizontal layers across the study area (Figure 5). As stated above, the reflectance for all opaque surfaces is 50 % and the light transmittance of glazing is 50 %. This is a simplified calculation of the quality of light distribution and the estimated light quantity which does not permit conclusions on the actual illuminance. However, a tendency – that is the daylight characteristics of the museum – is clearly discernible.

Distinct zones of daylight delivery to the collection spaces are made legible. Close to the glazed facade, up to a distance of approximately one third into the depth of the space, is a zone of high daylight availability. Here, the daylight factor exceeds 8–10 %, so that even on an overcast winter's day with external illumination levels of 10 000 lux, the projected interior illuminance is greater than 800 – 1 000 lx.

Daylight delivery is significantly reduced in the rear two thirds of the space. The daylight factor in the centre of the room is already below 2 %.

This initial general daylight simulation has shown that the "mythos" spaces receive a limited amount of daylight via the atrium and transitional zones close to the facade.

*Daylight study of "mythos" spaces*

The myth areas were designed displaying the characteristics of a dark theatre space without any noticeable influx of daylight. During the architect's and exhibition designer's early outline proposal stage this architectural concept was tested to determine whether it would be feasible in conjunction with the open sequence of spaces, and was later checked again in a detailed study. The zone receiving daylight extends only a few metres into the space. Disturbance of the intended dark theatre-like atmosphere is caused less by illuminance, i. e. the illumination of the space, than by the luminance, i. e. the brightness of the light apertures.

A further daylight simulation is used during the detailed proposal stage of the architects and the design of the exhibition space, the light transmittance t of the roof and facade glazing was set at 0.17 and the reflectance of opaque surfaces assessed according to the specifications of materials provided by the exhibition designers. For the highest altitude of the sun (21 June, noon) with a diffuse (overcast) sky, the simulation showed that the "mythos" spaces receive relatively low levels of daylight and thus – as intended – could be perceived as closed off "artificial lighting spaces".

*Shading study*

Architects, exhibition designers, artificial-lighting designers, HVAC engineers and even the landscape architects were interested in the data pertaining to how much of the building, or parts of it would be exposed to direct sunlight. A shading study was produced which incorporated neighbouring buildings and the elevated road to the east.

Simulations were carried out at hourly intervals for the day of the highest altitude of the sun (21 June), the lowest altitude of the sun (21 December) and the equinox (21 March and 21 September).

The design of daylight and artificial lighting at the New Mercedes Benz Museum in Stuttgart unifies two exhibition principles. It achieves both ideals, a museum flooded with daylight, along with the precise staging of single exhibits in a theatre-like setting. Light is an essential component of the expressive architecture of this museum.

13

## Light Control: a Part of Facility Management

ULRIKE BRANDI LICHT

Actuators
(receiver of
command)

230 V
BUS

Sensors
(sender of
1 command)

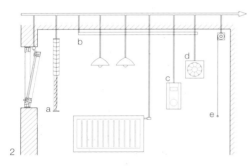

a   Light control
b   Cooling ceiling
c   Control unit
d   Ventilation
e   Screen

1   Design of EIB (European Installation Bus)
2   Bus system spanning different trades
3   Control systems of varying complexity for single
    rooms, storeys or building segments or compre-
    hensive "Building Management Systems" (BMS),
    (Source: DALI Manual)

Increasing expectations regarding comfort and security standards in buildings
require sophisticated measures for control of technical functions. At the same
time, operating costs should be reduced,
mainly by focussing on energy savings.
Here, the most important factors are the
control of lighting (daylight and artificial
light) and the room ambient temperature
(heating, cooling).
All measures employed for the efficient
operating of buildings can be summa-
rised under the heading of "facility management". The more these are attuned to
the interdependency and influence of
individual measures, the more effective
they are. Light and indoor climate control
systems were, until recently, generally
developed separately since they fall
under the expertise of different trades.
Now they are often combined.
These solutions are generally run on a
building-wide bus system, but less complex systems, for example room by room,
are also possible. To exploit all the advantages of all systems simultaneously cannot work, since there are too many ambiv-
alent factors (mainly in the field of thermal
loads and hence power consumption).

### Elements of power optimisation and comfort enhancement

The (intelligent) control of daylight man-
ages the delivery of daylight and anti-
glare devices.
- Controls on the facade are very effective. Systems are installed in front of the
  facade, often within the glazing, rarely
  in the interior.
- Adaptable skylights can be efficiently
  controlled as well.
- Finally, there are special devices, such
  as heliostats which direct light by following the path of the sun.

The (intelligent) control of artificial lighting
works with:

- Time-controlled systems utilising clock
  relays.
- Systems responding to the presence of
  people within a certain range by means
  of motion detectors.
- Artificial lighting control systems which
  have sensors to measure illuminance. If
  the threshold value is exceeded or falls
  below target, the luminous flux of the
  luminaire will be dimmed accordingly.
- Daylight dependant systems which
  have a sensor to measure outdoor illuminance; the lighting is dimmed accordingly, or switched off completely.

Indoor climate control also works with
sensors responding to internal and external temperatures, as well as other variables. Controls are designed with priorities
relating to the requirements of specific
buildings. Generally, the safety of the system has priority. For example, if weather
conditions are too windy, louvres or other
external daylight devices will be shut to
avoid damage. Systems often have additional settings for either the entire building
or certain sections of it. For buildings with
external daylight systems these could be
programmes for facade cleaning or system maintenance.
Furthermore, systems allow the control of
local functions such as interior lighting,
shading or individual indoor climate control. Users typically want a different setting in each room. The possibility of manual intervention is an important factor in
the acceptance of the control system. The
user should see it as a helpful device. His
particular choice interrupts the 'automatic
control' settings of the total system. So it
is important for energy balance how and
when individual settings are reset into the
optimised general system. Resetting the
intervention options of individual users
back into the total system is commonly
done (priority setting for the central basic
control):

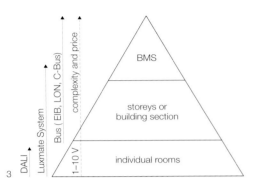

3

*(diagram labels: BMS; storeys or building section; individual rooms; complexity and price; Bus (EIB, LON, C-Bus); Luxmate System; DALI; 1–10 V)*

- at set times,
- at a certain period after the last manipulation,
- manually, for example by switching back onto "automatic operation".

## Control systems

Large-scale control of daylight and artificial lighting in buildings can be achieved using BUS systems (= Binary Unit System). Suitable systems have been on the market for approximately 15 years. They gradually replaced common conduit systems that branched out endlessly to bring electricity and power to each user in the building, providing the respective switching options via cables or different circuits. The more switching options, the more cables are required.

The bus system is a much better concept. All users are connected to the control via one single cable. This control configuration is independent of the power supply. Utilising a bus system will also save on installation costs because less wiring is required and there are no fitting costs. All bus components (these are the operating units, users or actuators and the instructors or sensors) communicate with one another via just one cable, provided that all components are bus compatible, i.e. electronically controllable.

Bus systems were initially developed for the traditional trades. Many manufacturers had, and still have, their own systems which are often incompatible. In the early "automated" buildings this resulted in many parallel systems – often using equal or similar components. Initial experience has led to the development of comprehensive systems for all trades (Figure 2). Now it is possible to incorporate almost all daylight and artificial lighting systems in one central system.

Because of the large number of tasks in a building and the high cost of extensive

"building automation", island solutions may be sensible, e. g. solely for artificial lighting, or for daylight control systems. Newly developed systems control just one room, with intelligent switches in the conventional sense. The bus compatibility of light fittings, for example, made it possible to control luminaires with single cordless switches via integrated infrared interfaces. This brings both cost and quality advantages regarding spatial flexibility. Walls that are repeatedly moved to accommodate the tenants' wishes are not compatible with central systems and cable runs, but portable luminaires are cheap when equipped with a sensor linked to the electronic ballast for daylight control, or dimming via an infrared switch. Here in the particular discipline of lighting, the maxim "small is beautiful, too" applies.

Popular, small manufacturer-specific control systems are Luxmate by Zumtobel, Light Scout by ERCO, and – generally manufacturer-independent – DALI, mainly used by Philips and AEG. The American company Lutron specialises in controls and operates throughout the world offering high-quality systems.

When deciding whether to install a control system for artificial lighting, the presence of other commercially available options for making significant power savings in commercial buildings, such as the use of energy-saving lamps, should always be considered. The actual energy balance of these lamps is controversial, but savings can be made simply because modern lamps have a much longer life than their predecessors of 15 years ago, when the bus systems were invented. Good facility management can also help to reduce maintenance, thereby saving resources. Finally, luminaires themselves are more efficient now. Their efficacy is much improved; it is easier to direct light and put it to specific uses.

Only the combination of carefully planned architecture and the selective use of technology in conjunction with a professional lighting design proposal for daylight and artificial lighting can lead to significant advantages in facility management.

Finally, three of the main control systems in current practice are briefly introduced.

*EIB (European Installation Bus)*
EIB is, next to the American LON, one of the most important bus systems on the market. The technology originated at Siemens and has been developed under the name of »Instabus« since 1987. Through ongoing development of the EIB technology, in collaboration with European partners, into the »Konnex (KNX)« standard, EIB/KNX now is the only system that complies with EN 50090, the European standard for installation bus systems.

Definition:
- EIB is a standard – not a product.
- EIB is an open standard bus (not manufacturer-related, approximately 5000 EIB product groups are available on the market).
- The advantage lies in its flexible installation, since switching options are achieved by reprogramming rather than rewiring.
- The involvement of all trades creates synergies that may reduce costs.

Data transfer / programming
- Bus lines transfer data between bus components.
- The standard for these data bus lines is paired cables with extra-low voltage 29 VDC routed separately from mains cables 230 V.
- In the version "Powerline" by EIB/KNX the 230 V mains may be used as data lines.

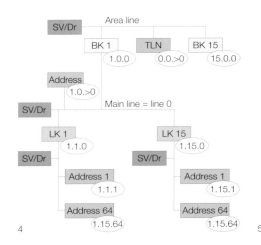

4

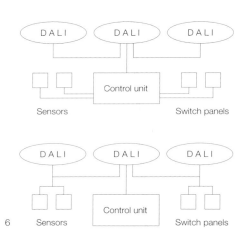

5

- Alternatively EIB/KNX can now communicate via wireless radio or infrared transmission.
- Decentralised intelligence – each bus component has its own microprocessor. There is no central device making the total breakdown of the system impossible.
- The system is programmed on a PC (link EIB to PC via interface RS232).

Bus components:
- Sensors: Sender command (e.g. keys, switches, motion detectors). These pick up physical (e.g. temperature) or digital variables (voltage), transform them into digital signals and send them via the bus link to the actuators.
- Actuators: Receivers of commands (e.g. relays, dimmers, drives). These receive signals from the bus lines and perform the relevant actions (Figure 1).

Addressing bus components:
- Each component has a physical address ("name" of component e.g. "3.5.8" = range 3, line 5, component 8; Figure 4).
- The group address determines the correlation, i.e. which sensor controls what actuator (e.g. motion sensor in toilets – dimmer luminaires in toilets).

Communication between bus components:
- Via telegrams. Each telegram consists of a series of 1 and 0 signals; the address field contains the source address and the destination address.
- CSMA/CA protocol (Carrier Sense Multiple Access/Collision Avoidance): All bus components listen, but only those addressed respond. If the bus line is free, it can transmit; if it is busy, it has to wait. If two commands are sent simultaneously the participant with higher priority prevails.

*LON (Local Operating Network)*
The bus system LON, developed by the company Echelon (USA), has been on the market since 1991. Its performance spectrum is similar to that of the EIB system. The choice of the appropriate system is assessed by a professional engineer. From the onset LON was designed for the combined control of heating, indoor climate and ventilation with other trades such as lighting, shading, visualisation, access control and elevator control (Figure 5). EIB, on the other hand, was developed for the traditional electronic domain of controlling light and blinds, and was only gradually enhanced to encompass tasks of different trades. The development history has resulted in a different "architecture" of the data networks EIB and LON. This has brought certain advantages for LON in dealing with large, complex buildings with complicated control requirements and numerous parameters. The higher data rate, superior expandability and flexibility of LON, on the other hand, requires a higher planning and programming input. Hence, EIB has distinct advantages for use in less complex jobs, especially for residential projects – also because its market penetration in this field of application is much larger.

*DALI – intelligent interface*
DALI (Digital Addressable Lighting Interface) has been available since 1999. Its predecessor was DSI (Digital Serial Interface). It was developed in collaboration with European manufacturers of electronic ballast (amongst others by Philips, Osram, Helvar, Tridonic, Trilux; Figure 6).

Definition:
- DALI is an international standard.
- DALI is applicable to light control only.
- DALI is the protocol for digital communication between components of a lighting system.

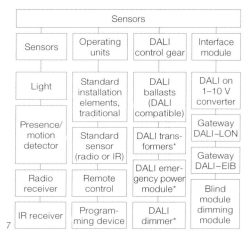

6

7

8a      b      c

- DALI facilitates multivendor-capable logic operation and control of intelligent luminaires (luminaire groups, light scenes).
- DALI is not a bus system, but an interface definition.
- The DALI standard is defined by the ballast standard IEC 60929, Appendix E.
- DALI is primarily a space-oriented light management system, its size is limited to 64 addresses.
- It is simple to operate and does not require much training.

Data transfer/programming:
- The DALI controller (master) controls the individual components (slaves): "master-slave" system.
- Data transfer is via a two-wire cable, extra low voltage of 22.5 VDC – this can be routed together with the mains.
- Addressing the components is done automatically on initial operation (connection of control module).

How many and what devices can DALI control?
- Electronic ballasts for fluorescent lamps and compact fluorescent lamps
- Electronic ballasts for discharge lamps
- Dimmer for incandescent lamps
- Transformers for low voltage halogen lamps
- Electronic ballasts for LED
- DALI is defined for a maximum of 64 single units (individual addresses) + a maximum of 16 groups (group addresses)
- DALI can be integrated into the primary building system technology, such as EIB, or LON via interface modules. This is done to control sections of large buildings and to communicate with other trades.

What can DALI do?
- Switch on and off
- Dim, recall light scenes (up to 16 per

DALI control device), information feedback (luminaire on/off, light level, faulty luminaire)
- Automatic search of control gear. Settings and light levels are saved directly to the DALI electronic ballast (individual address, group assignments, light scene settings, dimming speed, emergency lighting level, power on level)
- Synchronised dimming of several lighting circuits.

The question of which control system should best be used for what task, or if and to what extent the different systems can be combined or even integrated into a facility management concept on the strength of their performance and cost profiles, depends on the size and complexity of the requirements and the compatibility or availability of the respective terminals. Another consideration is how user-friendly the running of the system is and how easily the system can be modified.

4  Example of addressing EIB components: An area comprises the main line with a maximum of 15 line connections of 64 addresses each. Each area line, mainline and line requires a power supply (Source: EIBA).
5  Design of LON (Local Operating Network)
6  Design of DALI control systems (two alternatives): The control devices provide the logical allocation between sensors, control panel and DALI operating unit. This may be a stand-alone control device or an interface module receiving commands from a primary system. There also are intelligent sensors or operating units with integrated control devices.
7  Example for the components of a light control system operating on a DALI interface (*projected)
8  A traditional example of light management for the lighting of conference rooms. The light is adjusted to suit specific situations and requirements, e. g. meeting (Figure a), lecture (Figure b), presentation (Figure c).

# Procedure for Planning Artificial Light in Buildings

Christoph Geissmar-Brandi

## Prerequisite

Lighting design of interior spaces by professionals is a wholehearted, enjoyable pursuit. The result is the designed light ambience which has an effect on the well-being of the people who live and work or spend their free time in a building.
The development of a successful scheme can only be achieved by a team, and requires in-depth knowledge and good communication skills of all its members.

The aim of a good lighting proposal is to optimise in both technical and economic terms a scheme in combination with the following fundamental "vital" principles:

- Light reinforces the idea, the vision or soul of a space,
- the proposed light is compatible with the function of the building and meets expectations regarding the use of its interior spaces,
- the proposed system must be technically and economically optimised and thus within a reasonable budget,
- following the above three principles will ensure that the light is appropriate for the interior spaces, also in its respective details.

In essence this means that for each building project a new and individual solution must be developed in consultation with client, architects and electrical engineers, that puts into practice, to a high aesthetic standard, the functional and design objectives for the proposed building. The designed lighting system should be more economical than a standard solution, and should be made to last.

The lighting designer should consider several aspects, including

- light as a material, and
- light as a medium for visual communication.

Of equal importance is a comprehensive understanding of the entire building, its formal composition and technical systems, ceilings and facades, right down to the requirements and constraints of specific rooms.

Since lighting is often scheduled at the end of the design process, good communication between all the consultants involved, and mutual respect for each other's work, is essential. If communication fails, the often high expectations do not match the reality of costs.
When lighting designers are involved from the beginning of the design process, and when their wide experience of the effect of light on interior spaces (irrespective of the computable data) is utilised, their input can contribute significantly to the functional and spatial aesthetic optimisation of a building.

*Light as a material*
What we see is made visible by reflected light. Hence, the objective of a design proposal is not just light itself, but also the surfaces on which it falls. Information on the proposed surface materials and the reflective properties of floors, walls and ceilings is indispensable to the planning process; with it the designer can ascertain the brightness and the appearance of the room as well as its ambience.

The proposed colour scheme is a further important aspect to be considered in the design of lighting. Dark colours "swallow" light, bright hues are better in this respect as they reflect light. In the calculation of the size of a lighting system the effect of colour and reflective, or matt characteristics of a material, are still a matter of experience. Without this experience the designer tends to over-dimension the system to be on the safe side.

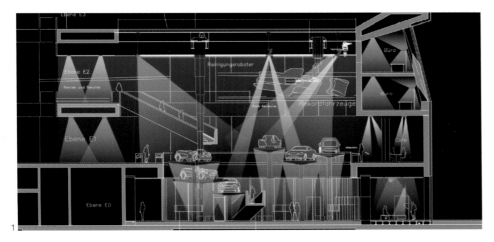

1    Design sketch of artificial lighting, atrium,
     New Mercedes Benz Museum, Stuttgart

*Light as a medium of visual (visible) communication*

Perception of our environment is very much influenced by the respective lighting conditions; light is one of the main factors in determining the atmosphere of a space.

In the assessment of buildings sophisticated lighting is considered as one of the "soft" qualities, which is not easily quantified, and, it may even be necessary to bring it to the client's or user's attention. The client's selection of a specific architect and a specific lighting designer, and his expectations with regard to their designs, communicate a specific intention. Whether it be a private investor, contractor or public institution, his choice conveys a whole spectrum of qualities such as openness or discretion, clarity, transparency, a feeling of security, respect for staff and guests and the wish for either innovation or tradition. The architecture will reveal these predilections. This could be described as "vibes"; the light responds, enhances and emphasises – architecture and light interact.

The following tools are available to the lighting designer:

- warm – cold light
- brilliant – diffuse light
- contrasting light (casting shadows) – soft light
- static light – movable light
- focussed light – general light
- daylight and artificial light
- in rare instances coloured light.

Different light ambiences of a room depend on changes in daylight and adjustments of the artificial lighting situation. Our (light) requirements differ; in the evening we want warm light, but during the day we can best concentrate in bright, clear, fresh and abundant light.

Lighting designers may have different opinions on how to handle light in buildings. They either integrate light into the architecture or seek visual dominance. The integrative approach prefers soft, sensitive light in all its nuances. The domineering approach demands strong, loud and colourful light. It is decorative, an accessory, sometimes contrived, often using appliquéd light objects. A third approach employs cool, anonymous light.

These approaches suit different architects, or rather their buildings. It is thus advisable for consultants who have compatible views to establish long-term working relationships.

**Tasks of the lighting designer**

First and foremost, lighting designers need to plan in cooperation with clients, architects, and various engineers; therefore technical know-how and competent design skills are required – and in fact both are necessary for good lighting design. The design of artificial lighting touches on all stages of the design process. It is thus important to have a systematic, step-by-step approach due to the often long time spans from commencement to completion. The result is not in evidence until the very end of the process when the building has been completed and it starts to "shine". It is only at this point that the expectations of the client, the architects and M & E engineers are fulfilled, the toil and limitation imposed by a small lighting budget forgotten.

Architects and clients define the building in terms of
- function and client/user requirements,
- interior space (height, width, depth),
- its relation to daylight,
- facade,
- surfaces of ceiling, walls and floor,
- colours, and

- standards of mechanical and electrical engineering, especially of electrical equipment.

The lighting designer's proposal is determined by
- light characteristics,
- light colours,
- light heights,
- light scenes,

in consideration of technical constraints that are based upon experience or on standards and regulations.

The components of the proposed lighting system are
- lamps,
- luminaries and reflectors,
- possibilities for their installation and future maintenance,
- circuit and wiring including ballast,
- circuit options, and
- emergency lighting.

**Design process**

In simplified terms, the lighting design process falls into a design stage and a production information stage. Planning permission is generally not required for lighting, except for proposals on facades (advertisements).

Initially, the design describes the light character and the type of lamp (for example, "indirect wash onto the ceiling"). The specification of the product and the setting-out of its location will be done at the production information stage.

Lighting tests play a central role in this context. They can be carried out on existing buildings (facade lighting), in show rooms or in mock-ups (1:1 simulations) at the manufacturer's offices. They are necessary for the correct assessment of proposed lighting effects. Considerable cost savings can be achieved by reducing systems that have been correctly calculated, but are in fact over-dimensioned, or by avoiding refitting or modification of a system at a later date.

*Scope of the appointment*
The degree to which the lighting consultant is involved beyond the concept stage, in the selection of products and the actual construction process, depends on the type and scope of his appointment. Contracts limited to design services are becoming increasingly widespread. The choice of product is then a question of cost, and will become the responsibility of the electrical engineers, rather than the task of the lighting designer. The outcome of his work depends on whether he was engaged as a lighting designer or as an adviser.

Lighting designers will produce CAD drawings for the entire building (auxiliary rooms and plant rooms are often omitted for practical reasons). The architects or the electrical engineers provide the plans onto which he adds the luminaires. The degree of accuracy of the positions and products shown on the plans depends on the progress of the job, and on the detail of the respective drawings. Early on, drawings will merely show the rough positions of luminaires; at the final stage, luminaires are accurately specified including information on accessories, quantities and on their setting-out.

As consultant, a lighting designer will develop a concept for either the entire building or for specific areas of that building. He will then discuss his outline proposal with the architects and engineers, and will make necessary adjustments. Illustrations are used to describe the intended lighting effect. At this concept stage the luminaire positions, heights and illuminance levels must be established; luminaire types and light colours are also stated, but the product itself is not yet

specified. It is not the role of the consultant lighting designer to draw plans necessary for construction. The "transfer" of the lighting proposal into the production information is the responsibility of the architects and engineers, as is the keeping to deadlines and budgets. To a large extent, the effective use of the lighting consultant's advisory service depends on their commitment and competence.

*Designing artificial light*
How does one proceed? Again, there is the question of the task as well as of individual skills. To find the appropriate lighting design solution for an exceptional building requires the trust of the client and architect, and usually a higher design input by the lighting consultant. Apart from such special jobs there are "normal" projects, generally presumed to be simple, that require the development of a professionally sound concept for specific rooms. These projects are often a challenge for lighting designers because they are run on tight construction budgets.

A good lighting design proposal is based on in-depth knowledge of the building. This can be difficult to achieve since clients

2

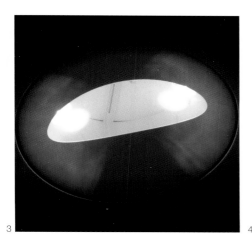
3

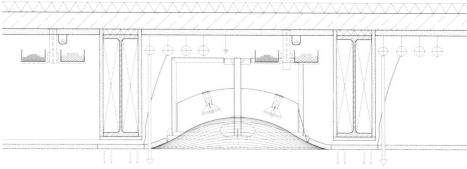
4

and architects sometimes have divergent expectations. They hire consultants to help with the technical realisation of their ideas, to openly discuss them or to enhance existing designs with the use of light.

The design process starts with an imaginary tour of the building. First of all lighting designers will, in their mind's eye, record the daylight apertures and the directions of users' views. Information on the building's siting is collected, also on the orientation of windows, neighbouring buildings, vegetation and the time of use. These activities are part of the preliminary services and the outline proposal stage. The design concept is defined once the proposed function of a space is combined with a lighting idea.

Most of the light we perceive is indirect light that is reflected onto the retina. The first step in the development of a design should be the assessment of the surface properties of the room. Its "furnishing" is also an important factor: a reading room has a certain type of light different from that of a hospital ward or a car museum. Light is specifically designed for different uses – even those within one room – taking into consideration the effect of colours and surfaces. In technical terms, this effect is measured as reflectance, a factor in the calculation of the necessary "light levels". In this way the first mental sketch of the design evolves.

Once the general idea of what areas need to be lit has been established, the rough positioning of the luminaires can be done and the luminaire types defined. The feasibility of these first ideas should be tested straight away. Proof of the expertise of a consultant lies in how far he is able to transpose a good design into a clear-cut system. If the design is feasible

in terms of ceilings, walls and floors, surface materials, cable runs, other aspects of M&E engineering, and apertures for windows and doors, then the necessary quantities of luminaires can be estimated and a rough calculation of the illuminance made. Generally, two to three different types of light will be employed, for example, vertical illumination, direct accent light and general illumination. The choice of luminaire depends on the type of lamp it operates. This interdependence arises from formal (aesthetic), technical and economic considerations.

Finally, the circuits, including switches and alternative controls for the different system options, need to be defined. Emergency lighting is designed concurrently.

Information on the types and quantities of luminaires, lamps and circuits, their installation and the required accessory devices is collected to produce a preliminary estimate of the proposal, and to work out its subsequent operating costs.

Irrespective of this, as the project progresses, it becomes increasingly important to make sure the scheme is within budget – and of course fundamental to the success of the concept.

A lighting designer who from the outset incorporates existing standards and regulations may also achieve good results. Generally, standards are recommendations, but in a commercial context and in conjunction with workplace directives, they are essentially binding. Other regulations, for example emergency lighting, must always be adhered to.

The final proposal stage entails the coordination of architects and engineers, and the presentation of the design to the client which then needs to be approved. Often the user, architect or the client requests amendments to the scheme

prior to approval. Amendments pose a problem for job profitability because it is generally expected that these are done at no additional cost to the client – and they can be time-consuming. Legal aspects of this problem are discussed in the section "The Lighting Designer's Position from a Contractual Point of View" (see pp. 84ff).

2–4 Photographs and drawings of the cloud luminaire for the ceiling of the collection area, New Mercedes Benz Museum, Stuttgart (see p. 57ff)
Architects: UN Studio van Berkel & Bos, Amsterdam
Daylight design: Transsolar Energietechnik and ULRIKE BRANDI LICHT

## Proposal and production information stages illustrated by examples

*Proposal: Pudong Airport, Shanghai*
The lighting design for the departure hall, part of the extension at Pudong Airport, Shanghai, exemplifies how lighting concepts can be developed, formulated and presented. Apart from the thoughts on design aspects outlined above, this includes the technical preconditions for the successful implementation of a proposal. Above all, the economic efficiency of the lighting system for a building of such dimensions must be considered.

Not only must the design be convincing in aesthetic terms, but must also fulfil the technical requirements of
- delivering the required illuminance,
- defining the luminaire positions to allow for easy installation and maintenance, and
- slotting into the construction sequence.

To convey all this to the parties involved is often difficult. Not many consultants can picture the effects of light. It takes good presentation drawings and apt images to convey a lighting proposal in a convincing manner.

Basically, a proposal is a typical sketch showing the direction of light and the light distribution. In the drawings for Pudong Airport colour was used to characterise different lighting zones.

It was proposed to light the departure hall indirectly via the roof. Good artificial lighting is not merely "bright" or "dark", but responds to the specific situation of the space, in this case a distinctly curving roof that is not uniformly but dynamically lit (Figure 5a).

Artificial lighting is employed to divide the vast hall into different zones. The counters, for example, receive direct light of a higher illuminance in response to their usage. The few walls in the open hall serve as "optical points of orientation", and thus receive stronger light.

At the beginning of a proposal one needs to be clear as to what is technically feasible. Once the consultant has done his – initially only estimated – calculations, he is confident and starts to look for suitable attachment points for luminaires and for possible luminaire types (Figure 5b). When these have been selected the proposal is tested – on the basis of the components (lamps) and light distribution of the luminaires and their reflectors – to determine whether it fulfils the requirements on brightness (Figure 5c). In this process the quantities of luminaires are established and their locations determined.

Off-the-shelf luminaires must be specified. Custom-made luminaires make for an interesting option in lighting design and may well be economically feasible for special functions. However, the retrofit or new construction of luminaires is not seen as part of the basic design services and should be subject to a separate fee agreement.

5 a–c Proposal, Departure Hall, Pudong Airport, Shanghai (under construction)
Architects: East China Architectural Design & Research Institute (ECADI), Shanghai
Lighting Design: ULRIKE BRANDI LICHT, Hamburg

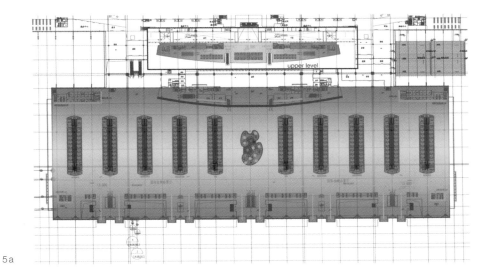

5a

Types of light
(direction and distribution)

indirect lighting

direct lighting

vertical
wall lighting

light panels

recessed floor
luminaire

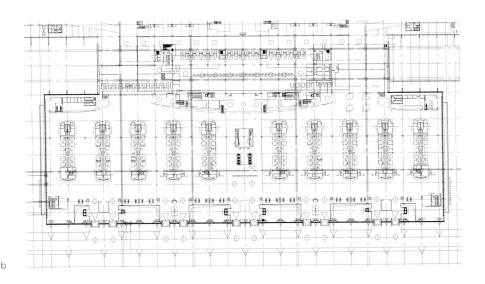

b

Types of luminaires

▽   pole luminaires

○   downlights

—   lighting of walls

– –  light panels

⊕   recessed floor luminaire

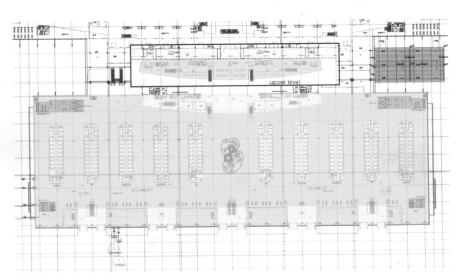

c

recessed floor luminaire

500 lx

300 lx

150–200 lx

6

*Production Information: Wellness Park
ELSE Club, Moscow*
In the Wellness Park Alissa visitors can
relax, exercise or meet various sporting
challenges. The lighting proposals
respond to both moods, not only in their
interior but also in their external appearance. The height at which luminaires are
mounted determines the atmosphere of a
space: low mounting heights make the
rooms look private and grand; light points
at mid-height on tables and in alcoves set
accents and create light islands.

The basic themes of the proposal are
"water" and "forest", both being elements
of the landscape in which people enjoy
relaxing and exercising. Just a few lighting principles tell a multifaceted "light
story", and create a pleasant and appeal-
ing ambience at the ELSE Club.

The detailed drawings were done in
AutoCAD using special (in-house) applications, at a scale of 1:100. For smaller
projects 1:50 may be a better scale. The
drawings are reflected ceiling plans.
They comprise all luminaire positions
and setting-out information. Each fixed
luminaire position is marked with a luminaire symbol representing its type. Special items (e.g. movable luminaires
including technical accessories or temporary luminaire positions) must be clearly
marked on the plan; this can be done
using coloured labels. If need be, luminaires can be labelled with an explana-
tory text listing irregularities (e.g. change
of mounting height). Whether the installation parts are to be noted on the plans or
in the specification should be decided in
advance.

The drawings should clearly distinguish
between emergency lighting and regular
luminaires.

High quality plans will also display a luminaire index in list form. The index lists all
parts featured including item numbers,
types, components, manufacturers, order
numbers, and (most importantly) the
quantities and respective plan symbols.
However, this is not the end of the production information stage for artificial
lighting; the performance profile also
includes construction details. These are
generally done at a scale of 1:10 or 1:5,
and describe installation and mounting
details, either drawn on A4 sheets or as
freehand sketches.

In the course of the professional detailed
proposal stage, the index on the plan is
developed into an illustrated list of luminaires in brochure format. This is referred
to as the luminaire book which will
include the specification and an illustration of each item. This compilation enables the client to assess the aesthetic and
functional aspects of the proposed luminaires; it is also an important control
instrument in the design process. It is
easier to discuss luminaires, or to pro-
pose alternatives, with the help of a luminaire book than by referring back to a
plan, and it can be quickly ascertained if
the proposed components (i. e. the
selected lamps) are cost-effective. In
some projects it makes sense to have
separate luminaire books for different
luminaire systems (such as regular luminaires, temporary luminaires, movable
luminaires, rental luminaires and emergency lighting).

**Tender action and contract preparation**
Everything the lighting designer has produced at the proposal and production
information stages, he now describes in
detail in the tender documentation stage.
Specifications for the trade "artificial
lighting" generally comprise all luminaires, including accessories such as

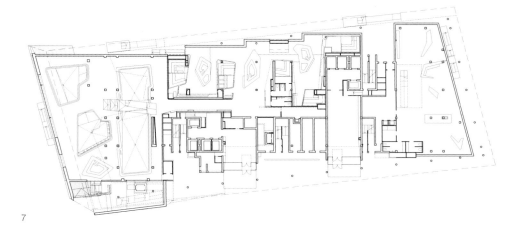

7

glare-controlling elements, filters, tracks
or poles. If the production information is
prepared thoroughly, the specification can
be developed straight from the luminaire
book. Daylight systems are, after consultation with the lighting designer, often
covered in the architect's specification.

The transferral of CAD data is achieved
via an interface in the database of the
specification programme, where, in turn,
interfaces are created for the import and
export of data by the tenderer. This information can be assessed in the form of
tender evaluation reports, or as single
items.

Until a valid EU directive stipulates the
division of construction costs of buildings,
this is governed by standard DIN 276 in
Germany. Lighting systems are listed
under the heading "High-voltage systems"
(4.5). They are further subdivided into
general lighting (4.5.1.0), special lighting
(4.5.2.0), emergency lighting (4.5.3.0)
and other lighting (4.5.9.0).

The lighting system can be treated as a
separate calculatory subsection within the
Electric Systems section of the specification. In this case the electrical engineer
will receive the texts from the lighting
designer. Alternatively, a separate specification for luminaires is produced, with
the possibility of a separate tender, since
luminaires are installed much later in the
construction process than other electrical
installations.
Luminaires are different from other building materials and fixtures required for the
construction of a building: while linear
metres of skirting board or cubic metres
of concrete can be specified irrespective
of a certain manufacturer, this is not so
easily done with luminaires. Even with
recessed downlights, which all look the
same at first glance, there are small but

significant variations in the products of
different manufacturers in the quality of
materials, the photometric data or the
appearance of installation rings. Hence,
clients often want the lighting designer to
specify a specific luminaire. Public sector
clients demand a non-manufacturer
related description of the luminaire. Per-
missible is the phrase "model luminaire
XY by manufacturer Z" but must include
the addition "or similar". It is the designer
who later has to test the equivalence of
the alternative luminaire.
The tender procedures may be subject to
different regulations. When the contract
sum exceeds a certain amount, German
public sector clients must accept tenders
from firms throughout Europe; national
and regional or invited tenders are used
for smaller contract sums. Only in a few
exceptional cases is a public client enti-
tled to award a contract without going
through the tender procedure.

6, 7 Lighting proposal and floor plan,
Wellness Park ELSE Club, Moscow, 2004
Architects: Architekturbüro 4a, Stuttgart
Lighting Design: ULRIKE BRANDI LICHT,
Hamburg

8

*Preliminaries to the specification*
The desired standard of quality for the lighting system and notes on the installation are dealt with in the "preliminaries" to the specification. These vary according to the type of project.

The profile describing the general standards of the Wellness Park ELSE Club:

"The implementation of the following services shall be understood as complete, including all accessories necessary for operation. Item descriptions contain binding information on luminaires.
All luminaires and devices must be constructed according to the regulations for the prevention of industrial accidents and the regulations of the Association of Electrical Engineering (VDE Verband der Elektrotechnik) or the relevant current version. All components must be of corrosion-resistant materials.
The client reserves the right, after inspecting the samples, to choose luminaires of different colours other than those listed in the specification.
All luminaires offered must be constructed according to DIN EN 12464 and VDE 0710 or DIN VDE O711 (equivalent to DIN EN 60 598), or be approved as of equal standard under the CCA scheme (Cenelec Certification Agreement). Additionally, all luminaires with first-time approval certificates by other certification bodies must be retrospectively approved by obtaining the VDE certificate in the course of the CCA scheme.

*Lamps*
The quality of lamps is expected to be equivalent to the products by the companies OSRAM or Philips. Discharge lamps should, if compatible with the components, be ceramic (HCI or CDM-T). Compact fluorescent lamps and fluorescent lamps should be warm white in colour.
If heat development necessitates luminaires for incandescent lamps should be wired up with silicone wires, connecting wires are to be covered in silicon tubes.

*Radio interference suppression*
All luminaires are to be specified to conform to the radio interference suppression value N.

*Safety isolating transformer*
According to VDE 0551/IEC 742, hum-reduced design, licensed for an ambient temperature limit of +40 °C, circuit breaker, voltage pick-up, dimmable, enclosure type IP 65, safety class II.

*Electronic transformer*
Safety transformers 10 to 50 VA according to VDE 0860/IEC 65, as well as 10 to 105 VA according to VDE 0871, licensed for an ambient temperature limit of +60 °C, dimmable.

*Ballast*
Ballast must display the VDE label. Dimensions of the ballast according to DIN 4985, nominal voltage 230 V, exchangeable, hum-reduced design. Unless otherwise specified, electric, dimmable ballast must always be used.

All luminaires are run on one installation bus. They must be suitable for operating on an installation bus and must be dimmable (also see Controls Specification).

8 Model, Wellness Park ELSE Club
In the Wellness Park visitors can relax, exercise or meet other sporting challenges. Both moods are reflected in the lighting proposals, in the interior and also on the exterior.

*Condensers*
Compensating condensers must be VDE approved and be certified fire-resistant and crack-resistant, discharge resistors and connection lugs must be insulated.

*Starter*
Safety starters.

*Wiring*
Pre-wired connections with "ready-for-use" wiring, factory-produced and attached to the housing, should be used (exception: systems described above). All wiring must be specified as not being susceptible to damage by any heat development of the ballast – also in the case of any malfunction. Push-connect terminal blocks (without screws) should be used for feed-through wiring, into which a non-metallic sheathed cable of up to $5 \times 2.5$ mm² can be inserted.
Design for external lighting or underwater lighting should be to the appropriate standards.

*Louvres and reflectors*
Louvres and reflectors should, if not otherwise stated, be of top grade aluminum (AL 99, 98), with a highly polished mirror finish. After shaping, the material is anodised on site to a layer thickness of approximately 10 μm. If highest-grade aluminum (AL 99, 98), band anodised, is required this must be explicitly stated in the specification. The quality of material selected should be without noticeable colour breakdown. If, instead of on-site anodised aluminum, a luminaire of a similar quality is offered, this must be specifically stated in the covering letter of the tender.
If the material is specified as AL 99, 85, the aluminum should be matt pre-anodised at 2 μm. Additionally, the material must be electro-polished.

A protective anodic coating is to be applied to make the surface touch-proof. Changes must not occur in the long-term. This also applies to the possible use of plastic reflectors.

*Division of services: materials/remuneration*
Delivery of all luminaires to the construction site is inclusive of carriage and packaging. The luminaire type must be clearly marked on the packaging.
Carriage charges must be itemised. For mirror-finish louvre units and luminaries with glass covers, the luminaire housing including fittings and mirror reflectors must be delivered separately. Alternatively, the mirror louvre may be delivered in dust-proof packaging and fitted in the luminaire in its wrapping during the ongoing construction work.
The tenderer must provide the client with samples free of charge.

*Preparing for luminaire installation*
Installation services of luminaries should include a previously prepared list of all necessary connections. This must be decided in consultation with the manufacturer and the technician installing the control system, and must be made available to all other relevant trades.
The division of services related to the fitting of luminaires is the connecting clip or the clip of the control gear. For external control gear, the contractor is responsible for both carrying out the necessary wiring and co-ordination with adjacent trades. Special care must be taken to coordinate works with the contractor installing the control system.

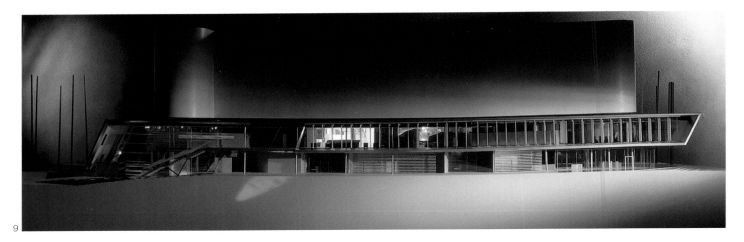

9

*Luminaire installation*
Luminaires delivered and stored on the building site should be unwrapped and installed, including all necessary alignment and adjustment work. If not under a different tender, this shall include connections, fittings and adjustment of lamps and starters, cleaning of luminaires prior to practical completion and testing along with all auxiliary services required for completion. Also included is the provision of all necessary equipment to be installed, provision of all necessary measuring equipment, delivery of all parts to be fitted or incidentals inclusive of installation costs covering both, installation instructions and supervision. Costs incurred from this should be part of the unit price.
Installation is to be carried out in coordination with other relevant trades.
Installation includes removal from site of packaging of luminaires and lamps, without request to do so by the site manager. This will not be paid for separately and is included in the installation cost for all items.

*Luminaire fixing*
Installation plans for the items should be prepared by the contractor, or checked by him directly after his appointment. The contractor has sole responsibility for the correct and safe mounting inclusive of all consequences that may result from incorrect mounting even after the defects liability period.

*Technical data*
On submitting the offer the tenderer must provide manufacturer's brochures or technical drawings, and the following technical characteristics in the form of test certificates:
· Coefficient of utilisation h (per cent)
· Glare rating according to DIN 5035 lengthwise/crosswise
· Luminous intensity distribution curve on the planes 0–180° and 90–270°.

*Example of an item in the specification*
The actual specification contains all luminaires and accessories as numbered items, such as the ones listed below:

Spotlight 04CD6503F-010 Manufacturer Ansorg Type CD R, or similar.

Spotlight for 3 spots on gimbal mounting for QR-LP111, 100 W, 42° angle of tilt in all directions.

Housing:
Recessed housing of galvanised steel, black. Aluminium spot and mounting frame, powder-coated silver.

Reflector:
Optional halogen reflector lamp, beam angle 4°, 8° or 24°.

Technical data:
ILCOS: HMGS/UB-111, external dimmable transformer 15 NE 9426, enclosure type IP 20, safety class III.

Installation:
On site preparation for installation: slit in the wall at a height of approximately 7 m.

With glass cover (on-site) according to drawing no. UBL-D002 (internal elevation and section).

Connected load per spot:
12 V, 100 W, control gear dimmable.

Dimension:
Width = 170 mm
Length (3× QR-LP111) = 480 mm

Luminaires to be delivered including all accessories, fastenings and lamps, installed and connected ready for use."

The example of a specification does not refer to a specific manufacturer. This is defined by the phrase "or similar" in the first sentence, after the manufacturer's name.
As in other trades, the lighting designer checks both the contents and figures in the tenders and produces one or more tender evaluation reports. He might advise the client at the tender meetings, or conduct them without the client since these reports are often used to resolve queries or to ask the contractor to add or elucidate items. Consultant and tenderer sign the meeting minutes which can be appended to the contract.
The consultant does not have to be present at the tender negotiation. If he is present, he can contribute to the price negotiations or help in their assessment.

9   Model, Wellness Park ELSE Club; swimming pool to the left and fitness area to the right

## Site inspection

The construction operations are error-prone because they are generally under a tight time schedule, many people are involved and the subject matter is complex. Difficulties can, for example, arise from design errors, poor coordination of trades, poor time management, errors made by contractors, missing deliveries and insolvency.

The primary aim of site inspection is to forestall mistakes, and also to ensure the smooth cooperation of all parties involved; crisis management is the second line of action.

Great care should be taken when defining the division of services between different trades at the level of both consultants and tradespeople, and when preparing the contract programme.

Ideally, the interface to the electrical engineer is the cable outlet; the luminaire is the responsibility of the lighting designer. Problems may arise if the luminaire is manufactured with a short length of wire. It must also be agreed who is responsible for the design of emergency lighting. Apart from the trade of electrical engineering (wiring, switches, controls) the following trades may well be involved: ceiling construction (apertures for recessed luminaires in plaster board ceilings), metal work (special fastening for the installation of luminaires to steel elements) and painters (gloss paint in colour of luminaire). The way in which these trades are implicated depends on the size of the construction project and on the individual trades.

The lighting designer must point out to the architect, who is responsible for the implementation programme, specific aspects inherent to his trade. Luminaires, for example, should not be installed before the paintwork has been finished. Equally, one would be reluctant to erect scaffolding for their installation on the finished flooring.

M & E engineers often carry out the site inspection for the discipline of lighting design. However, the lighting designer should visit the building site regularly – any insights gained will not only benefit the current project, but also future jobs.

Experience has shown that thoroughly prepared production information by the consultants is the best method to avoid errors at the construction stage.

The quality of drawings is important: symbols, keys, dimensions, additional information, direction of spotlights, references to detail drawings or sections, and cross-references to other subsections must be clearly legible at a glance.

Plans should always be approved by the architect before they are issued to contractors on site (deviations only with the client's or project manager's explicit and written instruction). This is the only way to ensure the contractor has both the latest and approved information.

In addition to the drawings there will always be verbal communication on site. Objectives can be discussed, improvements jointly worked on, misunderstandings avoided and problems solved. If verbal agreements relevant to the building process are made between the lighting designer and contractors, these, and any unresolved issues, should be noted in writing and initialled by all parties involved.

It is not easy to hit the right note, but it is the key to successful site inspection. In practice, each individual will find his own way of going about it. Cooperation makes the work enjoyable; it motivates both parties, and, in the end, the joy of a successful project can be shared by all.

Site inspection

10a    b    c

If an error should occur in spite of all the above procedures, it is important to find the right way to deal with it.

It is at this juncture that the client or his project manager has a great deal of influence. Projects in which the budget has been cut at the expense of quality, or in which the client is waiting for mistakes to occur so he can reduce costs, or when too much effort is spent on shifting the blame onto someone else, may all prohibit finding a solution to the problem. If one can be open with the client and participate in the process of damage limitation, good and practical solutions to the problem will generally be found. A client who is committed at a personal level is the best thing that can happen on a construction site, and subsequently to a building. On such occasions you often find that there is a great willingness to help others on the team.

Upon becoming aware of an error or delay, one should try to rectify the mistake as soon as possible. A consultant who tolerates an error is not performing his site inspection services in compliance with the contract.

The first legal tool for dealing with errors is to record the defect, the responsible party, and the date by which it must be rectified. If the defect has not been made good within the time limit, a warning is issued. Since the (lighting) consultant has no contractual relationship with the contractor, this is formally issued by the client or project manager, but initiated and worded by the consultant. The client can act on the ongoing refusal to perform, or incapacity to do so, by withholding monies or by appointing a third party to rectify the defect.

The consultant's next step would be the delay and disruption protocol. This informs the client in writing that another party is hindering the performance of a

service within the specified time period. According to the protocol the responsibility is passed from the person who should perform the service to the person who is delaying performance. Before any such measure is taken, all options to find a cooperative solution should be tested. But one must issue a written delay and disruption protocol if one's own schedule is in danger.

How to deal with notifications of defects and damages issued by the client is discussed in the section "The Lighting Designer's Position from a Contractual Point of View" (p. 84ff).

At the end of the building process the practical completion certificate is issued and a record of the condition of the works. This is the basis for the electrician's final account. Defects and provisos must be rectified within the time limitation on claims, or they will lead to a reduction of the account. It is in the lighting consultant's interest to see that defects are in fact rectified because he wants to see his design implemented as intended. Consultant and client are judged on what is built, not on why the results are not quite what they had in mind.

A special component of the lighting design discipline is the "lighting test", generally carried out at night towards the end of the construction stage. This is the fine adjustment of the positioning, orientation and control of luminaires in the nearly completed building. Here it is tested whether the light ambience corresponds to the original design intention. If everything is as expected, or even surpasses expectations, these impressions are among the best moments of the profession.

Galerie de L'Evolution, Paris, 1994
Architect: Chemetov + Huidobro, Paris
Scenography: René Allio, Paris
Lighting proposals: ULRIKE BRANDI LICHT, Hamburg
For the Natural History Museum at the Jardin des Plantes in Paris and its delicate exhibits in the main hall – the Parade of Animals in the centre – the lighting designers developed an artificial sky, the „ciel actif", which would imitate light ambiences from the outside world (daylight of the various continents at different times and seasons).
The initially proposed daylight ceiling (see p. 7) would have brought a variety of light ambiences of daylight into the interior of the building, but was substituted by an artificial lighting scheme in order to protect the exhibits.

10   a–c and right: Light ambience

for a potential claim for damages by the client if the cancellation turns out to be unjustified.

In his own interest and independently from problems having materialised in the contractual relation, the consultant should arrange for a carefully compiled written documentation of all agreements with the client, for example, instructions and concerns as well as relevant incidents on the construction site. For instance, the documentation may consist of minutes of meetings, memos and telephone notes, as well as correspondence with the client. In the interest of both parties, the consultant should ensure that possible disturbances and conflicts are recognised and resolved at an early stage during the duration of the contractual relationship. If conflicts can not be resolved out of court an extensive and diligently compiled documentation will help to enforce the consultant's rights in legal proceedings.

**Professional fees final invoice**

The contract's final invoice is of special significance. Due to the relatively complicated invoicing rules under the HOAI, the question of verifiability of professional fees final accounts is keeping a large number of courts very busy. However, as the falling due of the claim for professional fees depends on whether the fee note is verifiable (in addition to the services owed being in accordance with the contract and the receipt by the client of the final account) particular care should be had when drafting the professional fees final invoice.

The following is a short summary of the HOAI regulations on the invoicing of planning services. Because a large number of legal principles have been developed by the courts on the requirements of the consultant's final account it is, however, recommended to seek legal advice and assistance in each individual case.

*HOAI requirements*

The invoice must fulfil the HOAI requirements for the lighting design section (§ 69 et sec.). Pursuant to § 69 para. 1 the basis for the fees are admissible costs (§ 69 para. 3), the fee level (§§ 71, 72), the fee table (§ 74) as well as the services rendered and its valuation in percentage rates (§ 73).

In practice especially the correct assessment of admissible costs is a frequent source of mistakes. Admissible costs are determined and limited by the subject matter of the contract. With an expert consultant they follow the costs of his works and are to be assessed pursuant to the cost assessment methods of DIN 276 (April 1982 Edition). Under a comprehensive contract, therefore, the consultant has to supply a cost estimate, the cost calculation, an estimation, and cost findings. These different methods of evaluating costs are particularly distinguishable with regard to their accuracy because admissible costs will be determined with increasing precision as the project progresses.

Thereafter, the professional fees invoicing is done on the basis of the admissible costs, whereby the admissible costs for different performance phases must be determined by different cost finding methods. For example Service Phases 1 to 4 are being invoiced pursuant to the cost calculation (if not available, pursuant to the cost estimate), Service Phases 5 to 7 pursuant to the estimation (if not available, in accordance with the cost calculation) and Service Phases 8 and 9 pursuant to the cost findings (if not available, pursuant to estimation).

With regard to the determination of the fee level on the subject of lighting design the HOAI (§ 72 HOAI) distinguishes between lighting equipment pursuant to a calculation method based on the degree of effectiveness (Level II, average planning requirements) and lighting equipment pursuant to the point by point calculation method (Level III, high planning requirements). This subdivision appears to be technically outdated to the effect that in the area of today's lighting design, Fee Level III will generally apply.

Further relevant to the calculation of the professional fees is the fee table (§ 74 HOAI). It is sufficient in this context for the verification of the professional invoice to indicate the result of the interpolation; the process of interpolation itself does not have to be included in the invoice.

The final account must describe comprehensibly which works were performed in the individual case and include a valuation in percentage rates of the fee for basic services (§ 73 HOAI).

*Premature termination of the contract*

The verifiable invoicing of a prematurely terminated contract – mostly by cancellation – is very complex and legal supervision in each individual case highly recommended.

This applies in particular, when the contract was terminated by the client without reason (so-called "free" termination) as in this case the consultant can also charge for the work not done less disbursements saved and the deduction of possible other earnings alongside the works delivered (§ 649 BGB).

In this case the final account is to be subdivided into works delivered and works not delivered. With regard to the works not delivered it has to be explained comprehensively which costs (personnel costs and costs for material, general project-related costs) the consultant has actually saved because of the premature termination of the contract and if applicable, the amount of alternative income earned because of the premature termination of the contract.

*Proof of receipt*
Finally, the receipt of the professional fees final invoice by the client should be secured with the appropriate means (for example, by registered delivery). Pursuant to recent BGH leading cases the client can only raise objections to the final account's verifiability within two months from receipt of the invoice (BGH 27th November 2003, court reference number: VII ZA 288/02).

**In summary**
In addition to the demands accompanying providing services of a high standard, the consultant is also confronted with numerous legal challenges in relation to the planning project. The better the consultant is informed about his rights and obligations already in the run-up to his professional activities, the more likely costly and time-intensive problems can be avoided while carrying out the contract and/or disputes after the conclusion of the project.

---

[1] BGH = German Federal Supreme Court;
  Baurecht = construction journal 1997, page 154
[2] BGB = Bürgerliches Gesetzbuch i. e. German
  Civil Code

## Daylight as a Building Material

Merete Madsen
Peter Thule Kristensen

Daylight is one of the central themes of 20th century architecture. Daylight is not merely a means of bringing light into a building, or a traditional symbol of divinity; daylight is a building material in its own right that is celebrated in architecture. At the same time daylight is increasingly employed to create and dissolve space. Since the beginning of the century, space is no longer merely looked upon as a void surrounded by walls, but as something that stands alone – as infinite abundance. It is daylight that can shape an uncontoured space in an almost material way – just as it can make a fleeting ray of light turn an instant into an intense experience. The space takes on a peculiar meaning – as demonstrated in the paintings by the Danish artist Vilhelm Hammershøi (Figure 1).

In the same vein, the significance of daylight does not stem primarily from functional and physiological factors, as proclaimed by functionalism. In many of the major buildings of the 20th century daylight is also employed to create ambience and movement, to articulate the space in a new way.

As early as the 19th century values and symbols had become increasingly fleeting and the known system of the world, hitherto considered eternal, deteriorated; in architecture, traditional positions were called into question, as well. This was a challenge to architects' creativity, artistic energy and their urge to experiment – light and space were explored as independent phenomena.

It is interesting to trace how daylight turns into a "building material" that contributes to shaping modern spaces. What kinds of spaces are designed by daylight and its companion the shadow? How can daylight contribute to lending these spaces a special, spiritual atmosphere that is difficult to communicate in our fast-moving world and in the absence of a generally recognised, traditional or religious visual language?

The selection of the following European examples will illustrate how the building material daylight was discovered and utilised in the 20th century: in the buildings by Mies van der Rohe and Le Corbusier daylight is used to emphasise spatial complexity, with the help of reflection or by intricate interaction of several simultaneous light sources. In the works of other architects one can find examples in which sidelighting becomes a design element in its own right, or of broken light obtaining a spiritual character. We will see further examples of daylight used to localise places in an otherwise open interior space, or of cast shadows lending a sign-like character. Finally there are examples of how soft daylight can create almost weightless spaces. The projects are in chronological order, and conclude with an overview of current trends.

*Light reflex*

The characteristic of glass to create spatial links with transparency became an important design element of many 20th century architects. One source of inspiration was the industrial architecture of the 19th century with its new building materials and the resultant structural possibilities, such as steel construction making it possible to design large glazed areas. Glass can also reflect the surroundings and obscure the effects of light and shadow that otherwise emphasise space and form.

The German architect Mies van der Rohe utilised this effect. In his exhibition pavilion in Barcelona (1928–29) coloured glass walls form a strong, expressive element that filters daylight while reflecting the surroundings (Figure 2). In the pavilion, the characteristic of daylight to accentuate specific areas with cast shadows is of

1 "Dust motes dancing in sunlight", Vilhelm-
  Hammershøi, 1900
2 Light reflexes, German Pavilion,
  International Exhibition Barcelona, 1928–29;
  Architect: Ludwig Mies van der Rohe

less importance than exploiting daylight reflexes to create spatial ambiguity. Daylight is utilised to create an artful interplay of the coloured shadows cast by glass walls, reflections on glass surfaces, on the dyed natural stone walls, bare steel columns, and in a large pool of water. The changeability of daylight adds an extra layer to this simple yet spatially complex composition. When moving through the pavilion constantly changing views are revealed and reflections overlie spatial impressions – transparency and light reflexes create dissimilar and shifting spatial connections.

*Intersecting light*

The Barcelona Pavilion breaks with the traditions of classical design whereby the visitor obtains a general overview from the centre of the composition. Only by physically moving through the building can the visitor grasp the space in its entirety. The combination of space and movement is a theme of many 20th century architects, especially the Swiss architect and painter Le Corbusier, who liked to use daylight in arrangements of spatial ambiguity. These are rarely expressed in the form of daylight reflections on glass, but rather the interplay of competing sources of daylight that stimulate movement and create rooms with multi-faceted spaces and impressions.

This can also be seen in Le Corbusier's own apartment at the top of the Port Molitor Building in Paris (1931–34). In the foyer one can detect several daylight apertures: A cut-out in the ceiling above the stairs and a glass wall in the space beyond mark possible end points of intersecting lines of movement while a horizontal band of windows in the foyer underlines its passage-like character (Figure 3). The stairs are lit from different sides; the boundaries of the space are blurred. Light from the various apertures is superimposed when hitting the sculptural, free-standing, curved flight of stairs. The composition brings to mind a cubist painting in which the motif is observed from several viewpoints simultaneously.

*Sidelight*

The two examples from Barcelona and Paris represent an architectural style that uses daylight to stage a completely new form of spatial design. Architecture in Scandinavian countries is hardly ever this radical, but more attention is paid to utilising daylight as such; because Nordic light is less intense and thus a precious

building material. Northern architects have to work with diffuse, weak light that is generally emitted from an overcast sky. They consider light to be something special and use it accordingly; at times it borders on the spiritual or metaphysical.

One example is the funeral chapel in Turku, Finnland (1939–41) by the Finnish architect Erik Bryggman. In the middle of the day, a sidelight enters the chapel through a concealed opening and falls onto the back wall of the altar niche (Figure 4). Entering diagonally from above, it seems to belong to another world. Its religious character is emphasised by the fact that other light sources are visible. They either shine from below through the side aisles or through small openings in the dark vaults of the nave, which dramatically frame the bright altar niche. The sidelight is arranged as a changing "object", a substitute for the traditional altar screen. Through the side aisle one can see the tree trunks in the woodland outside, and thus the explicit focus on the altar is disrupted by an asymmetrical gesture. The worshipper is in a space between "mundane and heavenly" light.

3

3   Intersecting light, Apartment Le Corbusier, Paris,
    1931–34; Architect: Le Corbusier
4   Sidelight, Funeral Chapel, Turku, Finland,
    1939–41; Architect: Erik Bryggman

4

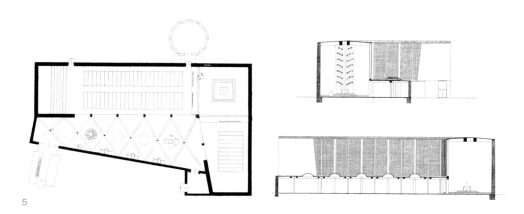

5

5 Floor plan, Section, St. Anna, Düren,
  1951–56; Architect: Rudolf Schwarz
6 Broken light, Nave, St. Anna, Düren
7 Localising light, Library, Rovaniemi,
  Finland, 1961–68; Architect: Alvar Aalto
8 Cast shadow, Gallaratese Residential Development, Milan, 1969; Architect: Aldo Rossi
9 Perspective, Facade; Gallaratese Residential
  Development, Milan

6

*Broken light*

Daylight also plays an important role for the German architect Rudolf Schwarz, in the design of religious spaces and the staging of their perception. For Schwarz the form principles of nature are mirrored in architecture. In this context Schwarz considers light to be the reverberation of a so-called "primary star" or "primary light", as a medium for the dialogue between the earthly and the heavenly. Building elements or objects, when illuminated, shine from within and become part of the primary light. One can recognise this dialogue in many of Rudolf Schwarz's churches, possibly most of all in his major work, St. Anna in Düren (1951–56).

Entering the low, dark side aisle from the street one can only surmise the nave beyond, with high stone walls bathed in mystic light. One wants to reach this light source and is drawn further into the nave, where a translucent glass wall, which dominates the space, is revealed (Figures 5, 6). It is not possible to obtain an overview as the nave and glass wall at the altar, the brightest place in the church, continue around the corner. This creates a dialogue between the large luminous glass plane and the stone wall opposite, which reflects the matt white light in a red glow. The treatment of light, using it to direct movement, and the design of the large glass wall as a profane industrial facade were trend setting for church architecture at the time. This sobriety stands in contrast to the other-worldliness of the red stone wall's broken light.

*Localising light*

The previous examples describe how daylight can be used to create spatial ambiguity or emphasise devotional meaning. Daylight can also be used to define particular locations in a space or to form specific areas. This is less about lighting effects as such, than about the space that is created though the use of light.

In the libraries designed by the Finnish architect Alvar Aalto, the daylight apertures are often designed and arranged in a way that quite naturally directs the visitors' attention to the books. In his library in Rovaniemi, Finland (1961–68) such use of daylight, by determining the spatial situation, is linked to a design language that appears to have been inspired by motifs and moods of the surrounding landscape (Figure 7). Daylight enters through a large opening in the roof, evenly illuminating the book shelves on the main floor. This area extends around numerous sunken

7

8

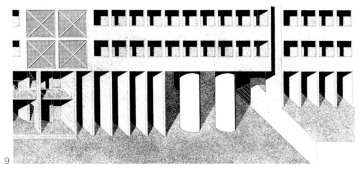

9

reading islands that are less brightly lit, yet spatially linked by daylight to the main floor. A skylight in the centre of the space picks out the lending barrier, marking this special situation.

Daylight emphasises a number of locations within the architectural landscape of this library, which is structured by alternating bright and dark areas. Aalto turns light into a space-forming building material.

*Cast shadow*

When 20th century architects attempted to communicate a metaphysical experience, they generally did this using light and shadow. This is clearly discernable in the work of the American architect Louis Kahn, who saw a close relationship between metaphysics, light, shadow and tranquillity, or the Italian architect Aldo Rossi, whose architecture was described as "speechless", possibly because he placed a significance on light and shadow.

Cast shadows play a similar symbolic role in the designs of Aldo Rossi as in the paintings of the Italian artist Giorgio di Chirico, some of which are bisected by a mystical shadow. Rossi's Gallaratese Residential Building outside Milan (1969), is structured by a high columned hall with even rows of concrete slabs that, in the course of a day, draw a changing pattern of cast shadows across the floor and

walls. The deep slit running through the building, and a level change in the building itself, make the columned hall appear fragmented (Figures 8, 9). This impression is further emphasised by the diagonal pattern of the shadows. Here shadow has a special significance: It emphasises the fragmented perception and lets the architectural forms (the over-dimensioned and empty columned hall) recede into the background. The shadow is cast and moves so slowly that time is arrested for one intense moment.

*Soft light*

Aldo Rossi uses light and cast shadow in a way typical of the architecture adapted to the glistening light of southern latitudes. As the Norwegian architect Sverre Fehn noted, cast shadows in the south show themselves even in a small crevice in a stone whereas the same crevice would remain unnoticed in northern light. Accordingly, Northern architects work with soft and reflecting daylight and its properties which create space and form. In this context the characteristics of the material and its colour nuances are an important theme.

In Bagsværd Church (1976) outside Copenhagen, it is precisely this kind of daylight that is utilised by the Danish architect Jørn Utzon who – inspired by the thought of an open-air church service beneath moving clouds on the coast – designed an ethereal church. From a

10

concealed opening, at the very top of the space, light slowly shimmers through the "cloud ceiling" consisting of a number of arched, bowl-shaped concrete elements (Figure 10). The soft curvature of the bowls and the material effect created by the imprint of the form boards reflect light without sharp contrasts and in many subtle nuances of grey – the ceiling appears to be floating. This impression is emphasised by the contrast of the precise cut-outs in the side walls that reveal the side aisles beyond, and their concrete frame construction. These areas are directly lit by skylights and are designed in bright nuances, similar to the other interiors. A whole universe of light – darkness does not seem to exist.

*Daylight as a contemporary building material*

The above examples illustrate how daylight was employed in 20th century architecture. Even today, at a time when it is possible to create artistic and daylight-like effects using artificial light, and when new types and variations of visual media attract our attention, daylight still is an important building material. It may be the result of this rivalry that the contemporary use of daylight has become somewhat more demonstrative or even mannered.

For the Jewish Museum in Berlin (2001) the Polish-born architect Daniel Libeskind, for example, designed daylight as a counter-pole to the "powers of darkness". In the darkest place of the museum, the Holocaust Tower, an out-of-reach slit is the only light source in this cold and dark space, while the Axis of Continuity, ending in a high and bright stairway, represents the hopeful continuation of Jewish history (Figure 13).

The Swiss architect Peter Zumthor treats daylight as an element that attracts attention. In his Kunsthaus in Bregenz (1997), the exhibition spaces are closed off to the sides but covered with a translucent glass ceiling. Daylight enters the building laterally, through areas in the facade between storeys, providing diffuse illumination in the exhibition spaces that extend across the entire floor (Figure 12). The rooms are kept so simple that unnaturally uniform, shimmering daylight is perceived as a phenomenon. This impression is emphasised by the fact that artificial lighting above the glazed ceiling discretely compensates for insufficient daylight levels, the illumination level in the room remaining constant at all times. Facades in sev-

11

10  Soft light, Bagsværd Church, Copenhagen, 1976; Architect: Jørn Utzon
11  Staged light, Fünf Höfe Shopping Centre, Munich, 2001; Architects: Herzog & de Meuron

eral layers effectively filtering daylight are a recurring theme of contemporary architecture. At Munich's Fünf Höfe Shopping Centre (2001), by Swiss architects Herzog & de Meuron, a version of coat of mail made of brown anodised aluminium, hangs curtain-like in front of parts of the facade (Figure 11). The daylight falling through the facade creates a lively pattern in the rooms behind – a clever effect achieved with the use of daylight as a building material.

In the three projects mentioned, the use of daylight does not produce a fundamentally different spatial concept. Libeskind uses daylight in the traditional, allegorical way to tell a specific story. Zumthor and Herzog & de Meuron seem to concentrate on the effect of daylight delivery. Light is filtered through several layers to reappear in a transformed state. In the latter two examples the night-time aspect of the facades incorporating artificial light is essential, a feature that can be found in numerous contemporary architectural projects.

Current developments seem to move towards a focus on the interplay of artificial light and daylight, or the staging of daylight and artificial light effects, rather than on daylight's potential to create space.

12  Staged light, Kunsthaus, Bregenz,
    1997; Architect: Peter Zumthor
13  Staged light, Axis of Continuation,
    Jewish Museum Berlin, 2001;
    Architect: Daniel Libeskind

12

13

Appendix

## Standards and Regulations (selection)

*Daylight and Artificial Light*

DIN 276: Building Costs

DIN 5030: Spectral measurement of radiation

DIN 5031: Optical radiation physics and illuminating engineering

DIN 5032: Photometry

DIN 5033: Colorimetry

DIN 5034: Daylight in interiors

DIN 5035: Artificial lighting; replaced by DIN EN 12464 Light and lighting – Lighting of work places

DIN 5036: Radiometric and photometric properties of materials, Part 1, 3 and 4

DIN 5037: Photometric evaluation of projectors, Supplement 1 and 2

DIN 5039: Light, lamps, luminaires – Definitions, Survey

DIN 5040
Luminaires (lighting fittings), Part 1–4

DIN 5042: Combustion lamps and gas luminaires, Part 1–8

DIN EN 12665, Publication date: 2002-09 Light and lighting – Basic terms and criteria for specifying lighting requirements

DIN EN 12193 Publication date: 1999-11 Light and lighting – Sports lighting

DIN EN 12464: Light and lighting – Lighting of work places;
Replaces DIN 5035-2, DIN 5035-8, DIN 5035-3, DIN 5035-4 and parts of DIN 5035-1, DIN 5035-7

DIN EN 13032-2 Publication date: 2005-03 Light and lighting – Measurement and presentation of photometric data of lamps and luminaires

*Daylight*

DIN 5034-1 Publication date: 1999-10 Daylight in interiors – Part 1: General requirements

DIN 5034-2 Publication date: 1985-02 Daylight in interiors – Part 2: Principles

DIN 5034-3 Publication date: 1994-09 Daylight in interiors – Part 3: Calculation

DIN 5034-4 Publication date: 1994-09 Daylight in interiors – Part 4: Simplified determination of minimum window sizes for dwellings

DIN 5034-5 Publication date: 1993-01 Daylight in interiors – Part 5: Measurement

DIN 5034-6 Publication date: 1995-06 Daylight in interiors – Part 6: Simplified determination of suitable dimensions for rooflights

*Artificial Light*

DIN VDE 0710-1 Publication date: 1969-03 Specifications for lighting fittings with service voltages below 1000 V; General requirements; Classification VDE 0710-1

DIN VDE 0711-201 Publication date: 1991-09 Luminaires; Part 2: Particular requirements; Section One: Fixed general purpose luminaires (IEC 60598-2-1 (1979) Edition 1 and Amendment 1 (1987))

DIN EN 410 Publication date: 1998-12 Glass in building – Determination of luminous and solar characteristics of glazing

DIN 5035-1
Terms and general requirements, partly replaced by DEN EN 12464

DIN 5035-2 Publication date: 1990-09 Artificial lighting; recommended values for lighting parameters for indoor and outdoor workspaces; replaced by DIN EN 12464

DIN 5035-3 Publication date: 1988-09 Artificial lighting of interiors; Hospitals; replaced by DIN EN 12464

DIN 5035-4 Publication date: 1983-02 Artificial lighting of interiors; special recommendations for lighting educational establishments;
replaced by DIN EN 12464

DIN 5035-5 Lighting applications – Emergency lighting; replaced by DIN EN 1838

DIN 5035-6 Publication date: 1990-12 Artificial lighting; Measurement and evaluation

DIN 5035-7 Publication date: 2004-08 Artificial Lighting - Part 7: Lighting of interiors with visual displays work stations; replaced by DIN EN 12464

DIN 5035-8 Publication date: 1994-05 Artificial lighting; special requirements for the lighting of single work-places in offices and similar rooms; replaced by DIN EN 12464

DIN 6169-1 Publication date: 1976-01 Colour rendering; general terms

DIN 6169-2 Publication date: 1976-02 Colour rendering; colour rendering properties of light sources in the field of lighting

DIN EN 12464-1 Publication date: 2003-03 Light and lighting – Lighting of work places – Part 1: Indoor work places

DIN EN 12464-2 Publication date: 2003-04 Light and lighting – Lighting of work places – Part 2: Outdoor work places

DIN EN 12665 Publication date: 2002-09 Light and lighting – Basic terms and criteria for specifying lighting requirements

DIN EN 12193 Publication date: 1999-11 Light and lighting – Sports lighting

DIN EN 13032-2 Publication date: 2005-03 Light and lighting – Measurement and presentation of photometric data of lamps and luminaires – Part 2: Presentation of data for indoor and outdoor work places

DIN EN 1838: Lighting applications – Emergency lighting

DIN EN 60598-2-24 Publication date: 1999-07
Luminaires – Part 2: Particular requirements; Section 24: Luminaires with limited surface temperatures (IEC 60598-2-24:1997, modified)

*Further information*

Verlag Beuth (publishing house)
www.beuth.de

Verein Deutscher Ingenieure
Association of German Engineers
VDI Guidelines
www.vdi.de

VDE Testing and Certification Institute
Standards Search
VDE Publishers
www.vde-verlag.de

## Bibliography (selection)

*Design with Daylight*

Baker, N.; Fanchiotti, A.; Steemers, K.: Daylighting in Architecture. A European Reference Book, London 1993

Binet, Hélène; Brandi, Ulrike; Bunschoten, Raoul; Flagge, Ingeborg; Geissmar-Brandi, Christoph; Schmal, Peter Cachola: The Secret of the Shadow. Light and Shadow in Architecture, Tübingen 2002

Boyce, Peter R.: Human Factors in Lighting, London 1981

Bundesamt für Energiewirtschaft Bern: Tageslichtnutzung in Gebäuden. DIANE Projekt Tageslichtnutzung, Band 1, (Swiss Federal Office of Energy: Daylight in Buildings. DIANE Project Daylight Utilisation, Vol. 1), Bern 1995

Bundesamt für Energiewirtschaft Bern: Systeme der Tageslichtnutzung. DIANE Projekt Tageslichtnutzung, Band 2, (Swiss Federal Office of Energy: Daylight Utilisation. DIANE Project Daylight Utilisation, Vol. 2), Bern 1995

Buonocore, Pablo; Critchley, Michael A.: Tageslicht in der Architektur, (Daylight in Architecture), Sulgen 2001

Çakir, Ahmet ; Çakir, Gisela; Kischkoweit-Lopin, Martin; Schultz, Volkher: Tageslicht nutzen. Bedeutung von Dachlichtöffnungen für Ergonomie, Architektur und Technik, (Utilising Daylight. Impact of Skylights on Ergonomics, Architecture and Technology), Bochum 2001

Epsten, Dagmar Becker: Tageslicht & Architektur. Möglichkeiten zur Energie-einsparung und Bereicherung der Lebensumwelt, (Daylight & Architecture: Potential Energy Savings and Enrichment of the Environment), Karlsruhe 1986

Evans, Benjamin H.: Daylight in Architecture, New York 1981

Flagge, Ingeborg: Architektur – Licht – Architektur, (Architecture – Light – Architecture), Stuttgart/Zurich 1991

Griefahn, Barbara: Perspektiven zur Gestaltung von Nachtarbeit durch Licht und Melatonin, (Perspectives of Designing Night Work with Light), Dortmund 2003

Hennings, D., et al: Leitfaden elektrische Energie im Hochbau. Vollständig über-arbeitete Fassung, (Code of Practice for Electric Energy in Buildings. Revised edition), Wiesbaden 2000

Köster, Helmut: Dynamic Daylight Architecture. Principles, Systems, Projects, Basel 2005

Kristensen, Peter Thule: Det sentimentalt moderne – Romantiske ledemotiver i det 20. århundredes bygningskunst, PhD., (The Sentimental Modern – Romantic Leitmotif for 20th Century Architecture), Royal Danish Academy of Fine Art, Copenhagen 2004

Lechner, Norbert: Heating, Cooling, Lighting. Design Methods for Architects, New York 2000

Madsen, Merete: Lysrum – som begreb og redskab (Light Space – Concept and Tool), Research Paper, Royal Danish Academy of Fine Art, Copenhagen 2002

Maffei, Lamberto; Fiorentini, Adriana: Das Bild im Kopf. Von der optischen Wahrnehmung zum Kunstwerk, (The Image in the Mind. Visual Perception of Artwork), Basel 1997

Müller, Helmut F. O.; Nolte, Christoph; Pasquay, Till: Klimagerechte Fassaden-technologie. Doppelfassaden für die Sanierung bestehender Gebäude, (Compatible Climatic Facade Technology. Double-envelope Facades for Refurbished Existing Buildings), Düsseldorf 2001

Muneer, T.; Gueymard, C.: Solar Radiation and Daylight Models, New York 2004

Niederländische Stiftung für Beleuchtungswissenschaft, Licht und Gesundheit für arbeitende Menschen, (Light and Health for the Working Population), Veenendaal 2003

Phillips, Derek: Daylighting. Natural Light in Architecture, Burlington 2004

Schwarz, Rudolf: Vom Bau der Kirche, Salzburg 1998; English Edition: The Church Incarnate, Chicago 1958

Stanjek, Klaus: Zwielicht. Die Ökologie der künstlichen Helligkeit, (Twilight. Ecology of Artificial Brightness), Munich 1989

VBG Verwaltungs-Berufsgenossenschaft (Ed.): Sonnenschutz im Büro, (Administrative Employers' Liability Insurance Association (Ed.): Sun Protection in Offices), Glückstadt 2002

Verein Deutscher Ingenieure (Ed.): Optimierung von Tageslichtnutzung und künstlicher Beleuchtung, (Association of German Engineers (Ed.): Optimisation of Daylight Utilisation and Artificial Lighting), Berlin 2002

*Journals*

Architectural Design, Light in Architecture, 67, 1997

a + u. Architecture and Urbanism, 1998/02

a + u. Architecture and Urbanism, Light in Japanese Architecture, 1995/06

Baumeister. Zeitschrift für Architektur, Kalter Stahl, (Cold Steel) 2005/01

Detail, Bauen mit Licht, (Building with Light), 2004/04

Der Architekt, Light and Order, 09, 1990

Daidalos, Lichtarchitektur, (Light Architecture), 27, 1988

LPI Leuchten Pro-in, Light for Vitality, 2004/03

Skala, Petri, Mathilde: Sverre Fehn, 23, 1990

Zumtobel Staff, Licht für Health & Care, (Light for Health & Care), Dornbirn 2003.

*Artificial Lighting*

Baer, Roland; Eckert, Martin; Gall, Dietrich: Beleuchtungstechnik. Grundlagen, (Lighting Technology. Principles), Berlin 2005

Brandi, Ulrike; Geissmar-Brandi, Christoph: Lightbook. The Practice of Lighting Design, Basel 2001

Bundesanstalt für Arbeitsschutz: Einflüsse der Beleuchtung mit Leuchtstofflampen am Arbeitsplatz, (Federal Institute for Occupational Safety and Health: Impact of Fluorescent Lamps at the Workplace), Bremerhaven 1991

Ganslandt, Rüdiger; Hofmann, Harald: Handbuch der Lichtplanung, (Manual of Lighting Design), Wiesbaden/Braunschweig 1992

Gfeller Corthésy, Roland: Bauen mit Tageslicht. Bauen mit Kunstlicht, (Building with Daylight. Building with Artificial Light), Braunschweig/Wiesbaden 1998

LiTG Deutsche Lichttechnische Gesellschaft e.V. (Ed.): Handbuch für Beleuchtung, (Lighting Manual), Landsberg 1991

Schröder, Gottfried: Technische Optik. Grundlagen und Anwendung, (Technical Optics. Principles and Application), Würzburg 1990

Schweizerische Lichttechnische Gesellschaft (Ed.): Handbuch für Beleuchtung, (Lighting Manual), Landsberg 1992

Smith, Fran Kellogg; Bertolone, Fred J.: Bringing Interiors to Light. The Principles and Practices of Lighting Design, New York 1986

Steffy, Gary R.: Architectural Lighting Design, New York 1990

Trilux (Ed.): Beleuchtungsplanung. Lichttechnik, Elektrotechnik, (Lighting Design. Lighting, Electrical Engineering), Arnsberg 1997

Weis, Bruno: Grundlagen der Beleuchtungstechnik, (Principles of Lighting Technology), Munich 2001

Weis, Bruno: Notbeleuchtung, (Emergency Lighting), Munich 1985

Zimmermann, Ralf: Wörterbuch Lichttechnik, (Dictionary of Lighting), Berlin 1990

*Facility Management*

Gröger, Achim: Gebäudeautomation, Renningen 2002

DALI AG, Fachverband Elektroleuchten im ZVEI: Handbuch: Digital Addressable Lighting Interface (DALI), (DALI AG, Activity Group ZVEI-Division Luminaires: Manual: Digital Addressable Lighting Interface), Frankfurt am Main 2002

**Further web sites**

BauNetz-Infoline: Light
www.baunetz.de/infoline/licht/

Fördergemeinschaft gutes Licht
www.fgl.de

Daylight in buildings
www.bine.info.de

Further links
www.daylight.org

Daylight design as PDF files available at
www.enermodal.com

*Light calculation programmes (selection)*

PRIMERO LICHT
www.al-ware.com
All light simulations mentioned in the chapter "Daylight – Characteristics and basic design principles" were produced using this programme.

Lightscape
www.autodesk.com

DIALux
www.dial.de

Europe DIAL
www.estia.ch

Radiance
www.radiance.com

Relux
www.relux.biz

*Institutions and Organisations*

European Lighting Designers Association ELDA
www.eldaplus.org

Fraunhofer Institute for Solar Energy Systems (ISE), Freiburg
www.ise.fhg.de

International Association of Lighting Designers IALD
www.iald.org

Institut für Fenstertechnik e.V. Institute for Window Technology Rosenheim
www.ift-rosenheim.de

Institut Wohnen und Umwelt GmbH Institute for Housing and Environment
www.iwu.de

VDI–Verein Deutscher Ingenieure e.V. Association of German Engineers
www.vdi.de

Zentralverband der Elektrotechnik- und Elektronikindustrie (ZVEI) e.V. Association of German Electrical and Electronics Industries
www.zvei.de

Verband Deutscher Elektrotechniker Association for Electrical, Electronic & Information Technologies
www.vde.de

Illuminating Engineering Society of North America (IESNA)
www.iesna.org

## Directory of Manufacturers of Daylight Systems (selection)

Products listed in brackets are generally only part of a comprehensive product range of the firm.

*Solar glazing*

Glaswerke Arnold GmbH + Co. KG
Alfred-Klingele-Straße 15
D–73630 Remshalden-Geradstetten
Tel.: +49 7151 70960
Fax: +49 7151 709690
service@glaswerke-arnold.de
www.glaswerke-arnold.de
(Thermal glazing, solar glazing, sound control glazing, fire-protection glazing)

BGT
Bischoff Glastechnik GmbH & Co. KG
Alexanderstraße 2
D–75015 Bretten
Tel.: +49 7252 5030
Fax: +49 7252 503283
www.bgt-bretten.de
(Luminous ceiling glass, colour-coated glass, etc.)

COLT
Internationale Solar Technology AG
Ruessenstraße 5
CH–6340 Baar
Tel.: +41 41 7685454
Fax: +41 41 7685455
www.coltinfo.ch
(Daylight technology, sun protection)

Flachglas MarkenKreis GmbH
Auf der Reihe 2
D–45884 Gelsenkirchen
Tel.: +49 209 913290
Fax: +49 209 9132929
www.markenkreis.de
(Thermal glazing, solar glazing, sound control glazing and safety glass)

OKALUX GmbH
Am Jöspershecklein 1
D–97828 Marktheidenfeld
Tel.: +49 9391 9000
Fax: +49 9391 900100
info@okalux.de
www.okalux.de
(Light-diffusing glass)

*Sun protection and anti-glare film*

AGERO AG
Hauptstraße 6
CH–8255 Schlattingen
Tel.: +41 52 6572611
Fax: +41 52 6573711
www.agero.ch
(Anti-glare devices)

Bomin Solar GmbH
Industriestraße 8–10
D–79541 Loerrach
Tel.: +49 7621 95960
Fax: +49 7621 54368
info@bomin-solar.de
www.bomin-solar.de

HAVERKAMP GmbH
Zum Kaiserbusch 26–28
D–48165 Münster
Tel.: +49 251 62 620
Fax: +49 251 62 6262
www.haverkamp.de
(Sun protection film)

Multifilm
Sonnen- und Blendschutz GmbH
Hohensteiner Straße 30 + 32
D–09212 Limach-Oberfrohna
Tel.: +49 3722 77050
Fax: +49 3722 770577
www.multifilm.de
(Sun protection and anti-glare film)

Saint Gobain Glass Deutschland GmbH
(formerly Vegla)
Viktoriaallee 3–5
D–52066 Aachen
Tel.: +49 241 5162221
Fax: +49 241 5162224
glassinfo.de@saint-gobain-glass.com
www.saint-gobain-glass.com

Saint Gobain Oberland
Division Bauglas
Solaris Glasbausteine
Siemensstraße 1
D–56422 Wirges
Tel.: +49 2602 6810
Fax: +49 2602 681416
info.solaris-glasstein@saint-gobain.com
www.solaris-glasstein.de

Schüco International KG
Karolinenstraße 1–15
D–33609 Bielefeld
Tel.: +49 521 7830
Fax: +49 521 783451
info@schueco.com
www.schueco.de

*Louvres and blinds*

GenioLux
Intelligente Lichtlenksysteme GmbH
Birostraße 6
A–1239 Wien
Tel.: +43 664 3409532
Fax: +43 2236 506683
Daylight@geniolux.com
www.geniolux.com
(Two pane insulating glass with inte-
grated light-directing mirror sections)

Glas Schuler GmbH & Co. KG
Ziegelstraße 23–25
D–91126 Rednitzhembach
Tel.: +49 9122 97560
Fax: +49 9122 975640
www.isolette.com
(Insulated glazing with integrated blinds)

Güth
Hamburger Landstraße 101
D–24113 Molfsee
Tel.: +49 431 650600 or 651942
Fax: +49 431 658225
www.gueth-molfsee.de
(Rolling shutters and blinds)

Hüppelux Sonnenschutzsysteme
GmbH & Co. KG
Cloppenburger Straße 200
D–26133 Oldenburg
Tel.: +49 441 4020
Fax: +49 441 402454
info@hueppelux.de
www.hueppelux.de
(Daylight-deflecting devices)

Köster Lichtplanung
Integrated Design for Daylight
and Artificial Light
Karl-Bieber-Höhe 15
D–60437 Frankfurt am Main
Tel.: +49 69 5074640
Fax: +49 69 5074650
info@koester-lichtplanung.de
www.koester-lichtplanung.de

Rosenheimer Glastechnik GmbH
Neue Straße 9
D–83071 Stephanskirchen
Tel.: +49 8031 9414830
Fax: +49 8031 9414848
www.rosenheimer-glastechnik.de
(Sun protection, screening, thermal
insulation)

SKS Stakusit Bautechnik GmbH
Eisenbahnstraße 2 B
D–47198 Duisburg-Homberg
Tel.: +49 2066 20040
Fax: +49 2066 2004164
www.sks-stakusit.de
(Rolling shutters, sun protection,
ventilation systems)

Siteco Beleuchtungstechnik GmbH
Georg-Simon-Ohm-Straße 50
D–83301 Traunreut
Tel.: +49 8669 330
Fax: +49 8669 33397
info@siteco.de
www.siteco.de

WAREMA Renkhoff GmbH
Vorderbergstraße 30
D–97828 Marktheidenfeld
Tel.: +49 9391 200
Fax: +49 9391 204299
www.warema.de
(Rolling shutters with daylight control)

*Light control glass*

INGLAS GmbH & Co. KG
Innovative Glass Systems
Im Winkel 4/1
D–88048 Friedrichshafen
Tel.: +49 7544 95470
Fax: +49 7544 954725
www.inglas.de
(Sun protection, anti-glare devices and
light control in glass)

Hüppelux Sonnenschutzsysteme
GmbH & Co.KG
Cloppenburger Straße 200
D–26133 Oldenburg
Tel.: +49 441 4020
Fax: +49 441 40454
info@hueppelux.de
www.hueppelux.de
(Daylight control)

*Prismatic sheets in double glazing*

Bomin Solar GmbH
Industriestraße 8–10
D–79541 Loerrach
Tel.: +49 7621 95960
Fax: +49 7621 54368
info@bomin-solar.de
www.bomin-solar.de

Siteco Beleuchtungstechnik GmbH
Georg-Simon-Ohm-Straße 50
D–83301 Traunreut
Tel.: +49 8669 330
Fax: +49 8669 33397
info@siteco.de
www.siteco.de

*Heliostats*

BatiBUS (France, Switzerland)
BatiBUS 11 rue Hamelin
F–75783 PARIS Cedex 16
Tel.: +33 476 394248
Fax: +33 476 394182
www.batibus.com

Interferenz Lichtsysteme GmbH
Lenenweg 27
D–47918 Tönisvorst
www.interferenz.de
(Light systems, luminaire development,
mirror-deflection systems, sunlight deflection using heliostats)

*Control systems*

Bomin Solar GmbH
Industriestraße 8–10
D–79541 Lörrach
Tel.: +49 7621 95960
Fax: +49 7621 54368
info@bomin-dolar.de
www. bomin-dolar.de

Crestron Germany GmbH
Ringstraße 1
D–89081 Ulm-Lehr
Tel.: +49 731 9628112
www.creston.de
(IT and media control systems)

EIB Control System
www.eib-home.de
Information page for electricians,
designers, architects and clients for
building management technology
with KNX/EIB

ISYnet/ISYglt
Seebacher GmbH
Building Automation
Marktstraße 57
D–83646 Bad Tölz
Tel.: +49 8041 77776
Fax: +49 8041 77772
info@seebacher.de
www.seebacher.de

LCN-BUS (Local Control Network)
ISSENDORFF Mikroelektronik GmbH
Wellweg 93
D–31157 SARSTEDT
Tel.: +49 5066 9980
Fax: +49 5066 998899
www.lcn.de

LON Control Systems
LON User Organisation
LNO c/o TEMA AG
Theaterstraße 74
D–52062 Aachen
Tel.: +49 241 8897036
Fax: +49 241 8897042
www.lno.de

Lutron Innovative Lichtsteuersysteme
Lutron Electronics GmbH
Landsbergerallee 201
D–13055 Berlin
Tel.: +49 30 97104590
Fax: +49 30 97104591
Lutrongermany@lutron.com
www.lutron.com

LUXMATE Controls GmbH
Schmelzhütterstraße 26
A–6850 Dornbirn
Tel.: +43 5572 5990
Fax: +43 5572 599699
luxmate@luxmate.co.at
www.luxmate.com

Somfy GmbH
Felix-Wankel-Straße 50
D–72108 Rotenburg am Neckar
Tel.: +49 7472 9300
Fax: +49 7472 9309
www.somfy.de

**Manufacturers Artificial Lighting
(selection)**

Products listed in brackets are generally
only part of a comprehensive product
range of the firm.

Ansorg GmbH
Solinger Straße 19
D–45481 Mülheim an der Ruhr
Tel.: +49 208 48460
Fax: +49 208 48461200
www.ansorg.de

Artemide GmbH
Hans-Böckler-Straße 2
D–58730 Fröndenberg
Tel.: +49 2373 9750
Fax: +49 2373 975209
pr@artemide.de
www.artemide.com

BEGA
D–58689 Menden
Postfach 31 60
Tel.: +49 2373 9660
Fax: +49 2373 966216
www.bega.de

Der Kluth
Herder Straße 83–85
D–40721 Hilden
Tel.: +49 2103 24830
Fax: +49 2103 248333
e-mail: info@derkluth.de
www.derkluth.de

Durlum
Decke Licht Raum
An der Wiese 5
D–79650 Schopfheim
Tel.: +49 7622 39050
Fax: +49 7622 390542
info@durlum.de
www.durlum.de

ERCO Leuchten GmbH
Postfach 24 60
Brockhauser Weg 80–82
D–58505 Lüdenscheid
Tel.: +49 2351 5510
Fax: +49 2351 551300
www.erco.com

Flos SpA
Via Angelo Faini, 2
I–25073 Bovezzo Brescia
Tel.: +39 030 24381
Fax: +39 030 2438250
expo@online.it

Fontana Arte spa
Via Alzaia Trieste 49
I–20094 Corsico
(Milano)
Tel.: +39 0245 121
Fax: +39 0245 12660
info@fontanaarte.it
www.fontanaarte.it

Grau
TOBIAS GRAU GmbH
Siemensstraße 35b
D–25462 Rellingen
Tel.: +49 4101 3700
Fax: +49 4101 3701000
www.tobias-grau.com

Hago Leuchten GmbH
Neckarstraße 4
D–45478 Mülheim an der Ruhr
Tel.: +49 208 5802530
Fax: +49 208 5802535
www.hago-leuchten.de

GUSTAV HAHN GmbH
Warmensteinacher Straße 56
D–12349 Berlin
Tel.: +49 30 76289040
Fax: +49 30 76289050
info@hahnlichtberlin.de
www.hahnlichtberlin.de

HELLUX LEUCHTEN GMBH
Lichttechnische Spezialfabrik
Mergenthalerstraße 6
D–30880 Laatzen
Tel.: +49 511 820100
Fax: +49 511 8201038
info@hellux.de
www.hellux.de

Hess Form + Licht
Schlachthausstraße 19–19/3
D-78050 Villingen-Schwenningen
Tel.: +49 7721 9200
Fax: +49 7721 920250
www.hess-form-licht.de

Hoffmeister Leuchten GmbH
Am Neuen Haus 4–10
D–58507 Lüdenscheid
Tel.: +49 2351 159318
Fax: +49 2351 159328
mail@hoffmeister.de
www.hoffmeister.de

idl
Leuchten und Lichttechnik GmbH
Annaberger Straße 73
D–09111 Chemnitz
Tel.: +49 3722 63100
Fax: +49 3722 87112
www.idl-leuchten.de
vertrieb@idl-leuchten.de

iGuzzini Illuminazione
Deutschland GmbH
Bunsenstraße 5
D–82152 Planegg
Tel.: +49 89 8569880
Fax: +49 89 85698833
www.iguzzini.de

Kreon nv
Frankrijklei 112
BE–2000 Antwerp
Tel.: +32 3231 2422
Fax: +32 3231 8896
www.kreon.com

LBM GmbH
Lichtleit-Fasertechnik
Gutenbergstraße 5
D–92334 Berching
Tel.: +49 8462 94190
Fax: +49 8462 941919
LBM@LBM-Fasertechnik.com
www.LBM-Fasertechnik.com

LEC LYON
6, rue de la Part-Dieu
F–69003 LYON
Tel.: +33 437 480409
Fax: +33 437 480411
www.lec.fr

Leipziger Leuchten GmbH
Heiterblickstraße 42
D–04347 Leipzig
Tel.: +49 341 245613
Fax: +49 341 2333151
www.leipziger-leuchten.com

Louis Poulsen & Co. GmbH
Westring 13
D–40721 Hilden
Tel.: +49 2103 9400
Fax: +49 2103 940290
      +49 2103 940291
www.louis-poulsen.de

Martin Architectural
Olof Palmes Allé 18
DK–8200  rhus N
Tel.: +45 87 400000
Fax: +45 87 400010
martinarchitectural@martin.dk
www.martin-architectural.com

MARTINI S.p.A.,
Industria per l'illuminazione
Via Provinciale, 24
I–41033 Concordia S/Secchia (MO)
Tel.: +39 535 48111
Fax: +39 535 48220
www.martini.it

NORKA
Norddeutsche Kunststoff- und
Elektrogesellschaft Stäcker
mbH & Co. KG
Sportallee 8
D–22335 Hamburg
Tel.: +49 40 5130090
Fax: +49 40 51300928
www.norka.de

Philips AEG Licht
Unternehmensbereich Licht
Steindamm 94
D–20099 Hamburg
Tel.: +49 40 28993366
Fax: +49 40 28992499
www.aeglicht.philips.de

Regent Beleuchtungskörper AG
Dornacherstraße 390
Postfach 246
CH–4018 Basel
Tel.: +41 61 3355111
Fax: +41 61 3355201
www.regent.ch

RSL
Tannenweg 1–3
D–53757 Sankt Augustin
Tel.: +49 2241 8610
Fax: +49 2241 334600
www.rsl.de

RZB Rudolf Zimmermann
Bamberg GmbH
Rheinstraße 16
D–96052 Bamberg
Tel.: +49 951 79090
Fax: +49 951 7909198
info@rzb-leuchten.de
www.rzb.de

SILL GMBH
Lichttechnische Spezialfabrik
Ritterstraße 9–10
D–10969 Berlin
Tel.: +49 30 6100050
Fax: +49 30 61000555
www.sill-lighting.com

Siteco Beleuchtungstechnik GmbH
Georg-Simon-Ohm-Straße 50
D–83301 Traunreut
Tel.: +49 8669 330
Fax: +49 8669 33397
info@siteco.de
www.siteco.de

Targetti
TARGETTI SANKEY SpA
Via Pratese, 164
I–50145 Florenz
Tel.: +39 055 37911
Fax: +39 055 3791266
www.targetti.com

Trilux TRILUX-LENZE GmbH + Co. KG
Heidestraße
D–59759 Arnsberg
Tel.: +49 2932 3010
Fax: +49 2932 301375
www.trilux.de

WE-EF LEUCHTEN GmbH & Co. KG
Töpinger Straße 19
D–29646 Bispingen
Tel.: +49 5194 9090
Fax: +49 5194 909299
www.we-ef.com

WILA Licht GmbH
Vödeweg 9–11
D–58638 Iserlohn
Tel.: +49 2371 8230
Fax: +49 2371 823200
www.wila.de

Willing – Dr. Ing. Willing GmbH
Columba-Schonath-Straße 4
D–96110 Scheßlitz
Tel.: +49 9542 92250
Fax: +49 9542 922528
www.willing-online.com

Zumtobel Staff
Schweizerstraße 30
A–6850 Dornbirn
Tel.: +43 5261 2120
Fax: +43 5261 2127777
info@zumtobelstaff.at
www.ZumtobelStaff.at

*other artificial light suppliers:*

Fördergemeinschaft Gutes Licht
(FGL)
Stresemannallee 19
D–60596 Frankfurt am Main
Tel.: +49 69 6302353
Fax: +49 69 6302317
fgl@zvei.org
www.licht.de

On-Light:
www.on-light.de

Appendix
Picture credits

## Picture Credits/Copyright: